How to Shield Children
from Alcohol and Other Drugs

To great mom Sandey
and the "Butch"

Angela L. Belec
7/13/08

How to Shield Children

from Alcohol and Other Drugs

A Vital Source of Knowledge for All Those
Involved in the Lives of Children

Angela R. Betances Ph.D.

TATE PUBLISHING & *Enterprises*

Published by Tate Publishing & Enterprises, LLC
127 E. Trade Center Terrace | Mustang, Oklahoma 73064 USA
1.888.361.9473 | www.tatepublishing.com

Tate Publishing is committed to excellence in the publishing industry. The company reflects the philosophy established by the founders, based on Psalm 68:11,
"The Lord gave the word and great was the company of those who published it."

Book design copyright © 2008 by Tate Publishing, LLC. All rights reserved.
Cover design by Jacob Crissup
Interior design by Jonathan Lindsey
Published in the United States of America

ISBN: 978-1-60462-902-6
1. Nonfict: Social Sit.: Drugs,Alcohol   2. Fam&Relationships: Adol.: Drugs/Dri
08.06.18

Dedication

I dedicate this unique book to the children of the world and to the memory of my only child, Anthony Nicholas Betances, whose high values, principles, and deep commitment against alcohol and other drugs inspired me to write *How to Shield Children from Alcohol and Other Drugs.*

Anthony was an honor student, recognized poet, all star-athlete, and a New Jersey State Governor's School Scholar. He was the recipient of many scholarships, including a medical research fellowship at the National Institute of Health in Bethesda, Maryland. Anthony researched the selective destruction of cancerous cells, a procedure presently used to treat leukemia. He graduated with honors from Cook College of Rutgers University, New Jersey, and was accepted by five medical schools. He elected to attend Thomas Jefferson Medical College of Philadelphia, Pennsylvania, to become a neurosurgeon. An automobile driver under the influence of chemical substance took my only child's life at the tender age of twenty-three.

Anthony had an outstanding *character*! He was a committed humanitarian focused on helping mankind. He campaigned for social and environmental issues, led groups to entertain children suffering from AIDS and cancer, fed the hungry, and formed anti-alcohol and drug advocacy clubs.

Anthony established a scholarship for needy students a year before his death, impelled by his strong belief that *a good mind should never be wasted for lack of money*. His scholarship is now endowed to perpetuity at Rutgers University of New Jersey.

May Anthony's exemplary character shine on all the children of the world, kindle their minds, and awaken their conscience to recognize the value and rewards of an alcohol- and drug-free life.

Contents

Introduction

Nothing can be more rewarding
And fulfilling in one's mind and soul
But the acknowledgment of
Saving a child from the abyss
Of drugs and alcohol!

—Author

How to Shield Children from Alcohol and Other Drugs is an informative and educational book for parents, caretakers, educators, and all those who are involved in the rearing and welfare of children.

The intent of this book is to inspire and encourage the readers to become strong and committed participants in the prevention of alcohol and drug use in children before it takes over their precious lives and consequently destroys their futures.

The concepts of this book are based and supported by existing scientific studies, research, and empirical data from diverse qualified professionals and institutions that have thoroughly studied and observed the negative affects of alcohol/drug use in children's lives. It is further reinforced by the writer's professional observation and experiences of twenty years as an educator, psychologist, and alcohol/drug counselor.

I sincerely believe that *How to Shield Children from Alcohol and Other Drugs,* through its factual, valid, and reliable scientific content and simplified style, will broaden the knowledge of readers and inspire them to become confident and dedicated teachers and advocates in the prevention and war against alcohol and drug use/abuse. It will give the readers appropriate and well-crafted tools that they may use with their children to build life-lasting anti-alcohol/drug foundations to broaden their horizons and instill confidence and courage to wholeheartedly commit their nurturing efforts to their children's welfare and happiness. Children tend to respect and trust parents, caretakers, teachers, and all those that are involved in their lives. Therefore, their inquisitive minds will be open and receive this work's wealthy and merited teaching that focuses on the development of healthy brains, minds, and bodies, free of alcohol/drugs and all other harmful behaviors.

This book may also serve as an educational merit resource to those individuals that are planning to enter parenthood. Thus, they will be prepared to shield their offsprings at a very young age from the alcohol/drug use invasion.

Furthermore, it will spare many parents, caretakers, educators, and society as a whole the hardships and devastating challenges set ahead from our children's possible involvement in the culture of alcohol and drugs.

Chapter 1

An Overview of Children and Adolescents: The Role of Rearing

If I save a child's mind
I would gain great pride
But if I save a child's life
I would touch the celestial sky!

—Author

Early Childhood Years

The word *children* has considerable latitude of meaning. *Webster's Dictionary* defines children as the immediate progeny of human parents; young persons of either sex, especially between infancy and youth. Children are also regarded as representing simplicity, innocence, trustfulness, and humility. Personally, I view children as a validation of the human existence reflecting on paramount challenges and rewards. I also believe that children are the most fragile flowers in the garden of the human world, which require a healthy and nurturing environment in order to blossom and sustain the changes of life.

Those that are involved in the study of children's growth and development, such as biologists, psychologists, sociologists, and others, unanimously agree that "child rearing" is a critical factor in both normal and abnormal human development and behavior across the life span. Healthy rearing has been researched and found to positively influence, in many cases, not only the early development of children, but also adult behavior. On the other hand, unhealthy rearing has shown to be associated with poor mental health and later alcohol and drug use and abuse (Baily & Kandel, 1993).

Children's early experiences (known as schemata) and their genetics are the milestones of their idiosyncratic persona. These two intertwined characteristics (schema), mainly manifestations of environment and genetics, are considered to be the most influential variables in children's early and later behavioral patterns.

The pertinence of schema in behavioral learning is strongly supported by Albert Bandura's Social Learning Theory (1969, 1977), which predisposes that people learn by observing the behaviors of others and the outcomes of those behaviors. Social learning principles affirm that people's cognitions, their perceptive views and expectations toward their environment affect their learning.

Based on these principles, children's first and mostly vivid experiences come from their home environment, parents, caretakers, and all other significant people that are in physical and emotional proximity to them. Such experiences may be positive or negative attitudes, beliefs, interests, hobbies, or festivities associated with alcohol and other drug use. Ultimately, they become permanent cognitions in the young minds of children and provide the architecture upon which life's behaviors will be built. Children's "critical thinking" in the early years of their lives is immature; subsequently, it deprives them of the capability to reverently judge a given situation and make the right decisions.

According to B.F. Skinner, renowned behaviorist, stimuli followed by internal and external reinforcement fortify behaviors encoded in the human mind. Children's brains, which grow rapidly in the early years of their lives, tend to be keen to environmental motivations and especially to those that come from parents, caretakers, teachers, and all others that convey trust, love, and admiration. Children are geared to learning, and the messages that they receive definitely are registered in their brain and chemical cells. Children's moral thinking, which is regulated by their level of intelligence, has not yet reached the developmental stage to differentiate healthy from unhealthy messages. Therefore, they are internalized, become part of their memory's repertoire, and are transmitted into behaviors and attitudes.

I would like to attest to the above declaration by elaborating on some of my troubled teen patients' verbalized experiences. For example, "I don't see anything wrong with drinking or smoking pot. My parents have been doing it since I can remember, and they are still here and okay. My parents work hard, are under pressure; they deserve to have fun and relaxation." These statements indicate that the children not only acquire parental alcohol/drug behaviors, but they also learn to use them to cope with stress, anxiety, and other emotional problems.

We cannot escape the reality that children are very engaged and intent on their parents' modeling. Therefore, we, as parents or caretakers, must compromise and sacrifice our personal desires, gratifications, and defense mechanisms, especially if they are directed toward alcohol and drug escapades. We must become the most repelling shields in our children's lives, which will protect them from the deadly bullets of alcohol and drugs. Chapter four of this book will provide an array of didactic and effective strategies and techniques that may inspire, help, guide, and navigate parents/caretakers and all those involved in children's rearing and welfare.

Adolescent Years

Recognizing the unique and complex entity of adolescent years, I find it necessary to familiarize the readers with the nature of adolescents and their susceptibility to alcohol/drug succumbing. It is important that we understand the teens' biological and psychological development and social context when we discuss alcohol/drug prevention.

In a simple description, adolescence is the stage of life between childhood and adulthood. It is a time where dramatic physical, emotional, cognitive, psychological, and social changes take place. The adolescents struggle to reconstruct a new image, one that will viaduct childhood perceptions to current ones. New feelings start to emerge during this stage, and some of them may be confusing and even frightening.

The founder of the scientific study of adolescence (Muus, 1996) describes the image of adolescence as a period of unavoidable "storm and stress." He writes, "There is no escape to their hurt, because their development is largely controlled by evolution and biology and thus generally unaffected by culture or context." On the other hand, Anna Freud, in her writings (1958) in order to emphasize the intertwining of stress and adolescence, states that adolescence without stress signifies a psychopathology. However, the current adolescence researchers unanimously agree that adolescence indeed is characterized by changes and great challenges. Nonetheless, adolescents should not be problematic and turbulent, pulled by the realm of their strong and perplex emotions and especially by a poor visual image (self-esteem). Self-esteem is not developed by miracle, but it is formulated and shaped by the interactions of parents, family, and the world in general. For example, if the self-esteem of a child has been nurtured by parental approval, recognition, praise, empathy, and understanding, the child is likely to feel self-worth. In the absence of all these, a child is likely to develop a weak sense of self integrated into his personality and is indivertibly unveiled throughout his adolescence and adult years.

Another cause of low self-esteem is the dynamics of the family. Through research and life experiences, we have discovered that children who live and are raised by alcoholics or drug users are harmed for life. These fragile children live in an intense, anxious, fearful, humiliating, and isolated environment because their families try to hide the problem. As a result, they feel anger, guilt, resentment, insecurity, uncertainty, deception, and many other unworthy feelings that are intertwined into their personalities.

As a result, they judge themselves harshly and often develop very low self-esteem, which governs their actions and behaviors throughout life. Furthermore, adolescents with low self-esteem have been found to have poorer mental and physical health, worse economic prospects, and high levels of criminal behavior, including alcohol/drug involvement, during adulthood compared to adolescents with high self-esteem.

In my professional career as school psychologist, I find a substantial number of children and adolescents having a history of poor self-esteem rooted in their family's alcohol/drug use and abuse. They feel inadequate in various social settings, tend to have a fewer or no friends at all, and are afraid to go to school because they view themselves as inferior. Many of these children/adolescents feel responsible for their parents' alcoholic problems and struggle with guilt from failing to save them from the effects of the disease of alcoholism. They are secretive and tend to conceal the truth in order to protect their parents' alcohol problem and save their family's pride. The younger children exhibit a low level of tolerance to their environmental stimuli, are hyperactive, and unable to remain still for a long time. The adolescents are easily frustrated, are aloof, angry, moody, and overly self-conscious.

Scientific research indicates that not only do drugs interfere with normal brain function by creating powerful feelings of pleasure, but they also have lasting effects on brain metabolism and activity (National Institute on Drug Abuse). Therefore, many of these young individuals are faced with serious psychological, emotional, scholastic, social, and alcohol/drug problems that threaten their existence and future. The Journal of Child Health USA reports that the annual prevalence of mental disorders in children and adolescents in the U.S. is about 25% percent, out of 78 million children and adolescents under age eighteen. Examples of such disorders may be anxiety disorder, simple phobia, obsessive compulsive disorders, panic disorders, mood disorders, disruptive disorders, cognitive impairment, and substance use disorder.

The Monitoring the Future Study (1975–1997), a long survey of the behaviors, attitudes, and values of American secondary school students, colleges, and young adults, found that 80 percent of adolescents have used alcohol by their senior year in high school and half of them have done so by eighth grade. Among all youths aged twelve to seventeen in 2004, 10.6 percent were current illicit drug users: 7.6 percent used marijuana, 3.6 percent used prescription-type drugs nonmedically, 1.2 percent used inhalants, 0.8 percent used hallucinogens, and 0.5 percent used cocaine (National Survey on Drug Use & Health, 2004). The latest study by the U.S. National Institute on Drug Abuse reports that nearly four out of every five students, 77 percent, have consumed alcohol (more than just a few sips) by the end of high school, and nearly 45 percent have done so by eighth grade. An estimate of 44.8 percent of marijuana and 11.4 percent of inhalants is reported for grades eight, ten, and twelve. For statistics of additional illicit drugs you may refer to Chapter 2 of this book.

Another aspect that has been considered as a major factor in the vulnerability of adolescents to alcohol and drug use/abuse is the genetic predisposition. The University of California, San Francisco Family Alcoholism Study, found that first-degree relatives of alcoholics are three to four times as likely to have alcoholism than the first-degree relatives of nonalcoholic. Twenty to twenty-five percent of sons and brothers of alcoholics become alcoholic, and 5 percent of daughters and sisters of alcoholics become alcoholics. Twin studies also indicated that identical twins who have exactly the same genes are more likely to be similar in having alcohol problems than fraternal twins who share half of their genetic materials. Even infant children of alcoholics that are adopted by nonalcoholic parents are still about three times more likely to have an alcohol problem although they were raised in a lower-risk environment.

The devastating effect of parental alcoholism can even be traced in the unborn child (fetus). Children born to alcoholic mothers are born with Fetal Alcohol Syndrome (FAS), one of the top three known causes of birth defects. About 5,000 babies are born each year with FAS, which causes facial and brain deformities and damage in the nervous system. Fetal Alcohol Syndrome and its effects are permanent and often lead to lifelong problems with mental retardation. The genetic link has been one of the most interesting areas in research and the findings in the Collaborative Study on the Genetics of Alcoholism are remarkable. Dr. Gordis states, "Researchers are making a concentrated effort to find the genes that are related to alcohol and other drugs.... No one is saying it is all genetic, but genetics play an important role." The most recent research indicates that genes on chromosomes one and seven are involved in alcoholism. With the completion of the human *genome* project in the next few years, the specific genes responsible for alcoholism will be identified. This will lead to the discovery of medications for predisposed individuals and more effective methods and techniques for alcohol abuse prevention. Some other studies have also identified greater levels of genetic interrelations with other drugs and nicotine dependency. However, the nature and the range of genetic predispositions call for extensive future research (Swan, 1999).

Although I recognize the salient role of family rearing and genetics in children's alcohol and drug involvement, I would not overlook other detrimental factors that affect the dynamics of the family, such as the death of a parent and divorce. The death of a parent, one of the most traumatic experiences in a child's life, like a volcano, spills out its lava over the body, mind, and soul and scars him/her for life. Death divests children from the parental unity that usually fosters a loving, caring, secure, and protective environment, significant prerequisites for normal human growth and development. Death anesthetizes the children's emotions and throws them into a stage of numbness, indifference, and despair. It affects their fragile psycho emotional world, which is flooded with powerful, painful, and perplexed feelings, i.e. abandonment, fear, sadness, sorrow, guilt, anger, anxiety, and even thoughts of suicide. Grieving children, in order to cope with such agonizing and overpowering emotions, manifest an array of diverse reactions depending on their age. For example, young children may experience regression, loss of speech, social withdrawal, sleeping, eating disorders, fearfulness, nightmares, temper tantrums, and increased dependency. School-age children exhibit deterioration of school performance due to loss of concentration, lack of motivation, and disinterest in school.

The adolescents' reactions are equally intense and dangerous. They exhibit depression, emotional detachment, withdrawal, school failure, somatic complaints, delinquent and promiscuous behaviors, and chemical substance use/abuse. Through literature and private practice, I have discovered that grieving adolescents, with a family alcohol/drug history, have a high risk to become chemical substance abusers after the death of a parent or a sibling. A large number of them, besides abusing alcohol and marijuana, eagerly indulge in prescription drugs that happened to be accessible in their homes.

The breaking of the family, one of the pestilences of our society, is a sensitive and devastating phenomenon that affects more than 58 percent of the U.S. children today. Divorce affects children no matter what age they are. They are at risk for developing angry and aggressive behaviors, sadness, depression, and impaired academic performance. The adolescents' reactive behaviors may be expressed in sexual acting out, running away, difficulty with intimate relationships, and alcohol/drug use and abuse. Working almost twenty years with children and adults in the mental and substance abuse field, I have a strong insight of the insidious impact of divorce on the lives of many individuals. Most of my young patients that are suffering from depression, social maladjustment, and substance abuse are still trapped in the painful experiences of their broken families. They are ambivalent, insecure, angry, aggressive, unremorseful, confused, aloof, and lost. It is obvious that divorce wounds children/adolescents for life, and alcohol and drugs appear to be one of the easiest ointments for their long-lasting pain.

I believe that through this chapter, the reader will harvest valuable information pertinent to the unique nature of children and adolescents. Furthermore, he/she will recognize that a healthy family and its positive modeling in the rearing of children can be the impermeable shield for alcohol/drug use. The next chapter will provide solid and basic information associated with alcohol and other prevalent drugs, which have become a haunting nightmare for all those that are responsible for the welfare of children and adolescents, as well as our society.

Chapter 2

The Truth about Alcohol and Other Drugs

Don't let the merciless drug
Seize my mind
I am your child, the essence
of your life!

—Author

Living in a chemically dominated society, I doubt if there is anyone that directly or indirectly did not have an experience with some sort of drugs. These may be prescribed or over-the-counter medications, recreational drugs, intentionally taken that change one's demeanor, or alcohol that many people do not consider it a drug. This chapter will focus on recreational drugs, including alcohol—the number one choice of our society—

cigarettes, and some abused prescribed medications, all of which are insidious invaders of our children's welfare and future. The information provided in this chapter is factual, scientifically researched, and experimentally proven. They will empower the readers and all those that are influential in children's lives with the knowledge needed to confidently discuss the truth about the hidden harm behind the deceiving pleasures of alcohol and drugs. The children will have the opportunity to learn the inevitable risks of alcohol and drugs from a very young age through credible people whom they love and trust. The internalizing of such knowledge will guide them throughout adolescence when they struggle for independence and identity and may easily seek recognition through poor choices, such as alcohol and drug involvement.

Before we discuss the various drugs, it will be wise to know what a *drug* is. A drug is any chemical substance taken into the body by mouth, inhaled, injected, or rubbed on the skin that causes changes in the body and/ or mind of the user. When the drug enters the body, it travels until it finds a molecule to attach to its receptor. Envision a drug as a type of key that fits into a specific lock (called *receptor*) of a cell. The drug remains on the receptor and alters the cell's function, resulting in physical, psychological, and emotional changes (Kuhn, C.; Swartzweider, S.; Wilson, W.; 2002). Drug use creates unnatural feelings. It causes the brain to change and remember intense feelings of pleasure, which makes the user crave more potent drugs in order to reach the highest euphoric plateau. In continuum, I will discuss the nature of alcohol and other recreational drugs and their multiple effects on the physical, psychoemotional, social, and educational world of adolescents.

Alcohol

Alcohol is a substance obtained from the fermentation of fruits, vegetables, or grains through purification and distillation. This fermentation occurs by the yeast cells acting upon the carbohydrates (sugars) of the plant to produce ethyl alcohol. The ethyl alcohol is the intoxicating element found in many substances, i.e., wine, beer, whisky, vodka, gin, rum, and some over-the-counter medications.

When alcohol is swallowed, it is not digested like food. It is absorbed by the mucosa lining of the mouth and enters the bloodstream via the stomach and small intestines. The alcohol remains there until the liver metabolizes it by oxidation. Ninety percent of the alcohol that enters the body is metabolized. If the amount of alcohol exceeds the liver's detoxication rate, the amount of alcohol in the bloodstream continues to increase, causing intoxication, brain impairment, coma, and possible death (TelMedPak, 2006). Alcohol is one of the biggest drug problems in our country and the number one killer among adolescents, greater than all other fatal illnesses combined (National Council on Alcohol and Drug Department of the San Fernando Valley, Inc., 2006). The perception that alcohol is socially accepted associates with the fact that more than 80 percent of the American youth consume alcohol before they reach their twenty-first birthday (U.S. Dept. of Health and Human Services, 2000). Alcohol has also proven to place adolescents in a higher risk for depression, given the fact that 3–8 percent of teens experience some sort of depression during adolescence (Costello et al., 1996; Kovacs, 1996; Lewinsohn, Clarke, Seeley, and Rohde, 1994).

Consequences of Alcohol and Drugs

The effects of alcohol are multi-dimensional, paramount, and perilous on young users, their families, and society. Underage drinking is a significant threat to our children's welfare and future. Research has proven that alcohol has a profound and persistent effect on children's/adolescents' physical and psychological development, even into adulthood. It also increases the risk of school failure, poor judgment, violence, unplanned and unsafe sex, and suicide (American Academy of Child and Adolescent Psychiatry, 2004)

Physical Effects of Alcohol—Alcohol depresses the central nervous system and consequently slows down the body's functions, such as heart rate and respiration. Lengthy use of alcohol destroys the liver cells and leads to cirrhosis of the liver, which is a fatal condition. Even small amounts of alcohol used for extended periods of time may destroy brain cells and result in cognitive deficits, severe memory impairment, and degenerative changes in the cerebellum, a region of the brain that plays an important role in the integration of sensory perception and motor production (Cerebellum, Wikipedia, 2006). Alcohol use is also responsible for cancer in the mouth, esophagus, stomach, and intestines. It also increases the risk for breast cancer, high blood pressure, kidney and heart disease, and strokes. It depresses the body's immune system and makes the user more prone to sickness.

Alcohol affects the brain, especially that of adolescents, which is sensitive because it continues to develop through childhood and adolescence up to about age twenty. Alcohol has been proven to cause anxiety, aggression, depression, confusion, and distortion of judgment, which is highly responsible for drunk driving. Drunk driving is a leading cause of death among teens predominately caused by motor vehicle accidents.

You can't imagine the unbearable pain and suffering those deaths brought to the families of those that have lost their beloved ones. As you may recall from the dedication of this book, I am one of the many grieving mothers who lost her only child, an ardent young anti-alcohol/drug advocate, who was killed by a driver that was under the influence of a chemical substance. According to the National Survey on Drug Use and Health's annual report, among the estimated 4.2 million young persons (aged sixteen to twenty) 21 percent have driven under the influence of alcohol. This is very alarming, and it should awaken the conscience of every parent/caretaker to make alcohol/drug education a prerequisite in his/her parenting mission.

Alcohol and other drugs change adolescents' attitudes and behaviors toward family, school, and society. When the families of my adolescent patients come to my center for family counseling, they are perplexed and frantic to find answers to questions such as: What is wrong with my child? What made him/her change from a caring, loving, and respectful child to an apathetic, indifferent, and defiant one? Why have my child's grades dropped so rapidly and now he/she gives excuses not to go to school? Perhaps some of the readers of this book may be pounded with the same queries and urgently search for some replies. I hope the following information enlightens the mind of the reader and many other parents/caretakers that are in such a quandary.

Effects on the Family—Family disintegration is another association with adolescents' alcohol/drug use and abuse. When families are invaded by their teens' alcohol/drug escapades, the entire family suffers. Parents and adolescents become more physically and psychologically distant from each other, and the peer relationships become more intense. Adolescents who generally do not recognize the consequences of their erratic and distractive behavior refuse to conform to their parents' guidance and pleas. Frequent conflicts and outbursts between parents and other siblings increase the family's strains and often lead to family disintegration. Inevitably, the place where previously peace and harmony prevailed now becomes a battlefield. This along with the astronomic expenses of the adolescents' drug treatment impose paramount economic pressures and hardships, which often cause serious health problems in the parents/caretakers and consequently affect their lives and the future of family members. Quite often, I treat mothers of teen substance users for depression, anxiety, and family relationships, especially custodian mothers who bear the responsibility of their children's rearing and the extra economic burden of a single-parent family.

Impact on School—Nearly four out of every five students have consumed alcohol by the end of high school according to the Monitoring the Future, National Results on Adolescent Drug Abuse report of 2003. These findings justify the SAMHSA, Office of Applied Studies reports, which indicate adolescents ages twelve to seventeen involved in alcohol and drugs exhibit changes in their grades and attitude toward school rules and regulations. Approximately 70.4 percent of those students' grades drop from As and Bs to Cs and Ds within less than six months after chemical substance involvement. Their participation in extracurricular activities, such as team sports, school band, Scouts, church, etc., declines, and their attendance suffers regardless of their parents' expectations. Furthermore, their behavior deteriorates due to suspensions related to school rule breaking and violations. During the period I served as substance awareness coordinator in the schools, I often witnessed students' behavior drastically change as soon as they became involved with alcohol and drugs. There were times that they fought in the school halls and playground, threw objects during class, smoked in the bathrooms, and vandalized school property. Most of them were under the influence of alcohol and drugs and consequently exercised poor judgment without recognizing the consequences of their actions and the impact on the future.

Impact on Society—Adolescents' substance use/abuse has a great impact on society's safety, economy, and welfare in general. The insensible underage drinking leads adolescents into delinquent activities and hazardous styles of life that not only threaten their personal safety and their families' homeostasis, but they also imperil the communities and cities where they live. The Counselor, The Magazine for Addiction Professionals, states that although the overall juvenile delinquency rates may have fallen in recent years, still the rate of incarcerated teens (ten to eighteen years old) has increased 291 percent within the last ten years due to alcohol and drugs. The poor judgment of the adolescent mind puts them at risk for accidents, violence, unplanned and unsafe sex, and crime. The Journal of the American Medical Association (1993) reported that fatal vehicle accidents at night are three times more likely to occur by teens, ages fifteen to twenty, who are under the influence of alcohol and drugs. The scope of juvenile violence goes beyond vehicle accidents. Homicide arrests, vandalism, drugs soliciting, gun trafficking, and other serious delinquent involvements such as theft and larceny are attributed to juvenile offenders (National Conference of State Legislator's Guide, 1996). Among twelve- to seventeen-year-old current drinkers, 31 percent had extreme levels of psychological distress, and 39 percent exhibited serious behavioral problems; sixteen- to twenty-year-old girls who are currently drinkers are four times more likely than their non-drinking peers to suffer from depression. In 2004, 5.7 million youths aged twelve to seventeen (22.5%) received treatment or counseling for emotional or behavior problems. Twenty-eight percent of the suicides by children ages nine to fifteen could be attributed to alcohol (Harwood, H., Fountain D., Livermore, G., 1998).

The Center for Disease Control and Prevention reports that the rise in cases of early-stage syphilis and chlamydia has dropped among adults the last three years from 29 percent to nearly 6 percent. Unfortunately, one group that is still at high risk for sexually transmitted diseases is teenagers. Inebriated adolescents often engage in audacious activities that expose them to sexually transmitted diseases, such as type B viral hepatitis, genital herpes, and AIDS, a life-threatening virus that is responsible for taking the lives of many young people. AIDS is caused by the Human Immunodeficiency Virus (HIV), which assails the blood's T cells that fight body infections. When the HIV invades the T cell, it prevents the cell from doing its job. Then it destroys the T cell by using the cell to make more viruses. Eventually, the new viruses swarm through the body, attacking and killing other T cells. Consequently, the organism is unable to defend itself against infections when sufficient T cells have been killed, and inevitably the patient becomes infected from other viruses, bacteria, and protozoa that he/she is exposed to. According to U.S. Centers for Disease Control, more than 38,490 young individuals age thirteen to twenty-four were diagnosed with AIDS in 2004. As we are aware, adolescence is a period during which young individuals engage in risk-taking and sensation-seeking behaviors. Alcohol and drugs, which alter judgment and decision-making, often lure adolescents in unsafe sexual behaviors that increase the chances of contracting AIDS.

Serious social losses also occur due to early alcohol/drug use. Their magnitude may be measured in the heavy financial burden imposed by the astronomic expenses associated with alcohol/drug treatment, lawful expenses, educational prevention programs, mental and physical illness associated with substance abuse and dependence, and economic declining, etc. The total cost attributable to the consequence of underage drinking is estimated to be more than 58 billion per year (Substance Abuse & Mental Health Services Administration, 1999).

Marijuana

Marijuana is a derivative from the Cannabis sativa plant, which grows in mild climates throughout the world. Its leaves and flowers are smoked, chewed, or eaten for their intoxicating effects. Marijuana contains more than 400 poisonous compounds, more than sixty cannabinoids, and many other ingredients. Marijuana's potency is due to the concentration of delta-9 tetrahydrocannobinol (THC). When THC enters the blood, it is stored in the fat tissues of the body, brain, cells, liver, lungs, kidney, and reproductive organs. Being an active poison, it prevents the formation of DNA, proteins, and other essential building blocks necessary for the growth of cells and their division. The effects of marijuana depend on the potency or strength of the THC chemical. Marijuana stays in one's system a few days after a smoking session and for weeks in the heavy user (National Institute on Drug Abuse, 2006). A recent study conducted in Europe among 2437 marijuana users concluded that there is a moderately increased risk for psychotic symptoms in young people, especially those with an above-average predisposition to psychosis. The "repetitious" exposure to marijuana may cause initial increases in synaptic dopamine and then lead to more prolonged changes in the endogenous cannabinoid systems. These changes are more predominant in individuals that used marijuana during adolescence (Henquet, C., et al., 2005).

Effects of Marijuana—Marijuana's effects depend on many factors: the dose taken, quality, frequency of exposure, previous experience with the drug, and how the drug is used. Studies show that regular use of marijuana may cause some types of cancer. Marijuana contains a number of chemicals found in tobacco smoke. Studies have shown that those that smoke five joints per day may take in as many cancer-causing chemicals as those that smoke a pack of cigarettes daily. The marijuana smokers develop respiratory problems, including lung infections like pneumonia. Furthermore, the THC in marijuana may attack the immune system by damaging the cells and tissues in the body, thus opening the body's susceptibility to infections (National Institute on Drugs Abuse, 1998).

Several studies have concluded that acute and long-term use of marijuana alters the secretion of hormones from the endocrine system. Testosterone and estrogen hormones, which are associated with the reproductive functions, were found to be affected by the use of marijuana, causing diminished sex drive and lower sperm counts. In addition, pregnant mothers may be vulnerable to change in hormone level, which can have an effect on offspring development. Children born to marijuana mothers are reported to experience increased behavioral problems during infancy and preschool years. These children are more likely to have problems with decision-making, short memory, and the ability to remain attentive (Cornelius, M.D and et al., 1995).

Recent research has recognized how marijuana affects the brain and alters its functions. There is a unique system in the brain, *cannabinoid receptor one*, found in many parts of the brain (cortex, hippocampus, basal ganglia, and cerebellum) and *cannabinoid receptor two*, found in the spleen. The cannabinoid receptors are part of the family of receptors for hormones and neurotransmitters. These receptors are in the parts of the cell that can change the way the neuron behaves. They may also regulate the way in which the neuron can release other neurotransmitters or interact with other neurotransmitters in the cell to produce a response. Several studies conclude that chronic and acute use of marijuana alters the secretion of hormones from the endocrine system, which may affect an individual's ability to respond to different metabolic changes and stress. Consequently, the individual experiences anxiety, depression, and panic. The abundance of cannabinoid receptors in the brain areas of cortex and hippocampus may alter the cognition level and effect short-term memory, mental activity, and motor functions, like altered reaction time and disruption of coordination (National Conference on Marijuana Use, 1995). I can attest to the altered cognition and marijuana or drug use/abuse factor. The last five years, being a school psychologist, I came across students whose IQ was average in their freshman high school year, but when I retested them two to three years later, I found their IQ to be low average or below average. Examining their behavioral records, I discovered high marijuana involvement as well as school suspensions and detentions. I urge readers if they notice their children declining academically and experiencing disciplinary problems at school to look into their children's lifestyles and immediately take action if they are involved with chemical substance use.

According to the Monitoring the Future Study, in the past twenty years more than one-half million young Americans have been surveyed. The results of this study indicated that marijuana continues to be a leading drug in the rebirth of the epidemic that started about twenty-five to thirty years ago with an increase in use among students grades eight to ten. Some studies support that the onset of drug use before age fifteen is an exceptional risk factor. The pattern of use is alcohol, tobacco, and then marijuana. Other studies indicated that 7 percent of the marijuana smokers use crack cocaine and heroin.

The science of behavioral pharmacology reports that marijuana also has a harmful impact on safe driving. Drivers under the influence of marijuana lack concentration, alertness, coordination, and reaction time. They tend to poorly misjudge distances and reaction to traffic signals. In a study in Memphis, Tennessee, of 150 reckless young drivers who were arrested for car accidents, 33 percent were positive for marijuana and 12 percent for both marijuana and cocaine. Data of drunk driver tests show that the lack of coordination among marijuana-smoking drivers is equal to those drivers that had too much to drink.

As you realize, I take great interest in providing information regarding the marijuana topic. I am extremely concerned that marijuana is not regarded as a dangerous drug by most users, their families, and society in general. I make this statement in clear conscience because a great number of my heroin and cocaine young patients, who are forced to engage in therapy by their parents, often say, "I should have continued smoking pot like everybody else smokes, including my parents." How do we expect our teens not to smoke pot when their parents model it? As long as marijuana use is prevalent in many teens' homes and its harmful effects are not known or denied, this insidious and crippling drug will not be included in the anti-drug war, and our children's sensitive brains will be vulnerable to heroin and crack.

Nicotine

Nicotine, one of the most toxic and addictive chemicals of the tobacco plant, is the most frequently used drug in the world. It is available in many forms, including cigarettes, cigars, chewing tobacco, snuff, gum, and even nicotine patches. The National Institute on Drug Abuse's own Monitoring the Future Study, an annual survey of drug use and related attitudes of America's adolescents, reported that since 1975 nicotine (in the form of cigarettes) has constantly been the substance that the greatest number of high school students use daily (National Institute on Drug Abuse, 2006).

The most important message that we should convey to our children is that nicotine is highly addictive. Its immediate effects dispel within minutes of ingestion. This prompts the user to frequent smoking throughout the day in order to maintain the drug's pleasurable effect and prevent withdrawal. Consequently, cigarettes' habit forming is rapid, and to refrain from it can be harder than alcohol or other drugs (Safety First, 2003). Repeated nicotine use results in tolerance development, which requires higher doses of the drug to produce the same initial stimulation. Chronic exposure to nicotine results in addiction whose cessation may cause serious symptoms that lead the user back to smoking. Some of these symptoms may be a persistent craving (the most lasting withdrawal symptom), cognitive and attention deficits, sleeping disturbance, and increase of appetite.

These conditions may last for long periods or a few days or weeks.

Consequences of Tobacco and Smoking—Tobacco use is estimated to kill at least 430,000 U.S. individuals yearly. This surpasses all deaths of heroin, homicide, suicide, car accidents, fire, and AIDS combined. People who smoke die earlier than those who do not smoke. The estimated costs accredited to direct and indirect smoking exceeds 138 billion dollars per year. An approximate 72 million young teens, ages twelve and older, use one or more tobacco products. Some of them might experiment for a short time, while others start a dangerous habit that may lead them to addiction and consequently to hazardous health problems, including premature death (Safety First, 2003).

The long-term smokers may develop cancer of the lungs, lips, stomach, kidneys, pancreas, cervix, bladder, and skin, heart disease, and stroke due to the nicotine and carbon monoxide contained in the cigarettes, as well as gastrointestinal problems related to excess acid in the stomach. High risk of bone fracture, wrinkling of the skin, sleeping and breathing problems, and decreased ability to play sports are also attributed to smoking. *Passive smoking*, the effect that smoking has on non-smokers, has the same risks as on those that smoke. It is estimated that passive smoking causes approximately 3,000 lung cancer deaths per year among nonsmokers and more than 40,000 deaths related to heart disease (Safety First, 2003). Children who are exposed to passive smoking have been diagnosed with more ear infections and respiratory problems than their counterparts.

The nicotine in cigarettes has stimulant and sedative effects. Therefore, smoking in adolescents may lead to a host of risky behaviors, such as unprotected sex and fighting, caused by the release of adrenaline through the adrenal glands stimulated by high nicotine. In addition, nicotine causes a release of dopamine in the brain, limbic system, which controls pleasure and motivation. This reaction is similar to other drugs, such as cocaine and heroin, and that elucidates the pleasurable feelings that the cigarette smokers experience. Research has found that nicotine is a highly addictive drug due to neurological changes during its development and maintenance. Some of these changes are tolerance and cessation of nicotine. Tolerance occurs when the nicotine is metabolized rapidly and disappears from the body within a few hours. Then, the user has to use it more often in order to be stimulated again. Cessation of nicotine is characterized by withdrawal expressed in irritability, craving, sleep disturbances, cognitive problems, and increase in appetite. These symptoms may last from a few weeks to six months (Loyola College, 2006). It is my vision that the presented information, as it pertains to the paramount risks and harms of nicotine and cigarette smoking, will enhance the readers' knowledge and reinforce their commitment to combat adolescents' smoking.

Cocaine

According to the William Gladden Foundation Library, cocaine is made from the leaf of the coca plant and is a hydrochloride salt. Originally, cocaine was used as an anesthetic by the medical field and later for other medical applications. In the late 1800s and early 1900s, the non-medical use of cocaine was widely spread in America. Some users chemically process cocaine and remove the hydrochloride. This process is known as "freebasing" and makes the drug more potent. Cocaine is illegally sold in three forms: cocoa paste, cocaine powder, and crack (a crystallized form of cocaine that is suitable for smoking). Cocaine can be injected into the veins, smoked, or snorted.

Cocaine is the most addictive drug, and its use has grown dramatically throughout the United States. Cocaine use occurs in every age level or social stratum, from teens to adults and from underprivileged to privileged. Laboratory researchers have discovered that cocaine dependence is very powerful. Crack cocaine has been described as a drug that delivers the users to a stage of pleasure that is outside the realm of their human experiences. In the meantime, this parody leads them into a world of torture and even death.

Psychological and Emotional Effects—Cocaine can affect the dopamine transport system in the reward pathway of the brain, including the limbic system, and alter its functioning. Emotionally and psychologically, chronic users of cocaine may feel irritability, anxiety, depression, memory loss, and mental confusion, lack of sex drive, and violent behavior. In addition, they experience *formication* (hallucinations of insects crawling underneath their skin), delirium, and paranoid psychosis. The neural aftereffects of the chronic cocaine use include changes in monoamine metabolites and uptake transporters. There is a down-regulation of dopamine D2 receptors in order to compensate for their drug-induced overstimulation. Consequently, the brain's capacity to experience pleasure is diminished, and users experience a dysphoric crash.

Physical Effects—Research suggests that chronic cocaine use is associated with medical problems, such as damage to the heart and cerebral blood vessels due to elevation of blood pressure, heart rate acceleration, and tension of muscles. When it is snorted, it may constrict the blood vessels and cause nosebleeds (perforated nasal septum); it carries the risk of infection with AIDS or hepatitis and adverse reactions to impurities. Death even from small doses can occur, which is usually caused by seizures or heart attacks. It is hard to save the user from cocaine overdose due to its rapid deadly effect. Death due to the overdose of cocaine is typified by tachycardia, erratic respiration, chills, vomiting, rise in body temperature, convulsions, hallucinations, delirium, and unconsciousness. Delirium is associated with a degenerate state, violence, exaggerated strength, hyperthemia, cardiac arrest, and sudden death (Drugs and Human Performance Fact Sheets, 2006).

Performance Effects—Low doses of cocaine use have shown some enhancement in attention, but no enhancement in learning, memory, and other cognitive processes were noticed. Harmful effects were noticed after exposure to high doses, chronic ingestions, and during withdrawal of the drug. Among those deleterious effects are agitation, inability to focus on tasks and to follow directions, confusion, time distortion, and poor coordination. Signs of impairment in driving performance have been reported due to poor inattentive and aggressive driving and poor impulse control. Among the 253 fatal driving incidents in Wayne County, Michigan, 10 percent of the drivers were under the influence of cocaine (National Traffic Safety Administration, 2006).

Social Effects—The social effects of cocaine users can be equally devastating. When I counsel families of cocaine users, I can see and feel the great agony and fear experienced as they are discussing their child's destructive behavior and attitude. They often state, "My child was such a loving, caring, respectful, and responsible person, how can he/she be so apathetic, dishonest, disrespectful, ruthless, and irresponsible toward his/her parents, siblings, relatives, friends, and school staff?" These behavioral characteristics are strongly reinforced by researchers who often found the cocaine users to be alienated from their families and healthy social interactions because they invest most of their time and energy in their compulsive and obsessive habit (Responsible Parent's Guide, 2006). We often see many cocaine users reject their family's love, betray their beloved ones, and threaten the entire community with their delinquent behaviors, i.e., lying, cheating, stealing, fighting, vandalizing, raping, and committing other serious violent crimes.

What deeply perturbs me is that many children today are experimenting with cocaine and crack. A 2004 National Institute of Drugs and Alcohol funded study reported that eighth to twelfth graders have tried cocaine at least once. The following represents an estimate of cocaine users—3.4 percent of eighth graders, 5.4 percent of the tenth graders, and 8.1 percent of the twelfth graders. These findings are serious and extremely alarming because they demonstrate that many of our young people indeed place themselves in a highly physical and emotional risk without recognizing the precarious outcomes. Therefore, we, as parents/caretakers and educators, must be well-versed in this subject in order to provide our children with reliable factual information that will have a profound impact on their impressive minds and serve as an armor in their long lives. Thus, we will not only save our children, but we will also spare ourselves and society from the pain, suffering, and paramount financial burden resulting from our children's cocaine/crack involvement as well as all other recreational drugs.

Heroin

Heroin is opium, like morphine and codeine. It comes from the opium poppy plant and is the most powerful narcotic drug. It appears as a white, off white, or brown crystal powder. Pure heroin is made from morphine treated with acetic acid (the acid in vinegar). Heroin acts upon the nervous system and the brain. Within the nervous system, brainstem, and spinal cord are receptors on the nerve cells that recognize heroin and other opiates. These receptors trigger responses in the brain and body. Heroin changes the limbic system of the brain to produce increased feelings of pleasure, relaxation, and satisfaction. In the brainstem, where automatic functions are taking place, like coughing and breathing, heroin can slow down or stop them. Surprisingly, there are natural receptors in the brain known as endogenous (delta, mu, and kappa). They produce chemicals that act like opiates, which control pain so the organism may survive under traumatic conditions. However, the brain cells know at what time and how much of these natural chemicals to use. Individuals that use opiates recreationally, like heroin, often use much more than the brain would release even under the most intense circumstances. This may cause an increase in pleasure and relaxation, and the individuals may become dependent on them (National Institute on Drug Abuse, 2006).

Effects—The majority of drug/alcohol researchers agree that all recreational chemical substances, including alcohol, in general affect the personality of the user. However, there are some researchers who reported that they found higher rates of antisocial personality disorders among heroin addicts and greater levels of psychopathology and maladaptation. In the Minnesota Multi-Personality Inventory, opiate users scored significantly higher than other drugs on the hypochondriasis (fear or idea of having serious diseases), depression, hysteria, psychopathic deviance, psychastemia (a neurosis characterized by anxiety reactions, obsessions, and fixed ideas) and schizophrenia. In addition, opiate users exhibited characteristics of isolation, associability or rebellion, and manipulation (Spotts, J.V., & Shnontz, F.C., 1983). The heroin users tend to interchange alcohol with heroin. In the addiction stage, they increase heroin use, and during the treatment period of heroin, they increase the use of alcohol. Teens who are involved in the use of this powerful drug experience substantial disruption in educational goals and develop a deviant identity (Anglin, M.D., et al., 1989).

Hallucinogens

Historically, hallucinogens have been part of human cultures for millennia through spiritual (rite of passage) and healing rituals. Hallucinogenic drugs are both naturally occurring and synthetically manufactured in laboratories throughout the modern world. Plants that contain psychoactive substances are: marijuana, peyote, nutmeg, belladonna, locoweed, jimson weed, mandrake, and varieties of morning glory seeds. Illegal hallucinogens include ketamine, mescaline, psilocybin (mushrooms), MDMA (an amphetamine, called Ecstasy), PCP (phencyclidine, also called Angel Dust), and LSD (called Acid). These drugs change the brain's ability to transmit nerve impulses. As a result, the mind alters perception of time and space and generates vivid and colorful images and illusions. Some scientists, like Timothy Leary and Richard Alpert, psychologists of Harvard University, found these experiences intriguing, and they contributed the *mind expending* to the psilocy-bin's and LSD's deceiving capability. On the contrary, some other users found the same experiences to be *mind wandering*, immeasurably frantic, and potentially self-injurious with long-lasting psycho-emotional distur-bances (William Gladden Foundation Library, 2006).

How Hallucinogens Affect the User—The 1991 National Institute of Drugs and Alcohol (NIDA) sta-tistics reported that 13 to 17 million individuals in the U.S. have used a hallucinogen at least once, seven to eight times more than heroin. The hallucinogens' effect is powerful and unpredictable on the brain. For exam-ple, they may make some people to hallucinate and become aggressive and dangerous, while others may become drowsy and passive. Hallucinogens distort the way the human senses function and alter the perception of time and space. They are orally taken, and the onset of the drugs is relatively slow. In the inception the users feel nauseous, dizzy, and anxious, and then their vision is distorted and feelings of unreality follow.

Since the hallucinogen drugs cannot be categorized into groups or one single drug, in this chapter we will discuss the most familiar and widely used hallucino-gens by young adults. The Department of Pediatrics at Fairfax Hospital in Virginia urges all doctors to consider the possibility of hallucinogens use when they evaluate delirious or psychotic adolescents. In a study group of 174 substance abusers, they found forty-five, 26 percent, to have used psilocybin (or mushrooms) together with alcohol. They concluded that the acute adverse reac-tions were related to the drug synergy—hallucinogenic psilocybin mushrooms and alcohol. LSD or Acid, psilocybin (mushrooms), DMT (dimethyltryptamine), mescaline (peyote cactus derivative), PCP or Angel Dust (Phencyclidine), and MDMA or Ecstasy have become the mostly popular psychedelic drugs used by many adolescents and young adults.

LSD or ACID (Lysergic Acid Diethylamide)

LSD or ACID is the most commonly used hallucinogen drug. Generally, it is taken by ingesting small strips of paper (placed under the tongue) previously soaked in the liquid of the drug and in some cases in tablets, liquid, and gelatin. Because LSD is an illegal product, the potency of its dose is difficult to be determined. Its effects begin about thirty minutes after ingestion and continue up to twelve hours. LSD, like mescaline and psilocybin (mushrooms), distorts the users' sense of reality and makes them delirious. These hallucinations may be pleasurable and thought-provoking for some individuals, but for others disorienting or distressing, causing a negative emotional experience, known as *bad trip*. As a result, the users may experience frightening thoughts and feelings, despair, and even fear of death. Failing to recognize the reality of their situation, some LSD trips end in fatal accidents. LSD affects the nerve cells by acting upon the serotonin receptors and altering their metabolic process. As a result, tumbling, insomnia, raised heart rate and blood pressure may occur (Brown University, 2004).

Long-term LSD users experience repetitious flash-backs for a long period of time after they quit the use of the drug, persistent violent behavior, anxiety, or distorted perception of time. During my internship for my drug and alcohol license, I came across a few chronic LSD patients who suffered from severe depression and schizophrenia-like syndromes. At times, they spoke about visualizing irresolute images and trails of colorful lights. Some of them were even diagnosed with psychosis. Furthermore, they started using LSD when attending college. Although this is an extremely disturbing awareness, it is also a realization to the need of continuous anti-drug/alcohol education for our children in order to brand into their vulnerable minds the value of a healthy body and mind throughout life.

MDMA or Ecstasy (methylenedioxymethamphetamine)

Ecstasy and MDA belong to the category of *enactogens* because they have hallucinogenic and mood-improving properties. Ecstasy originally was used for mental health treatment and as a dietetic aid. Its illegal use started in the late 1980s and early 1990s. This drug is widely used among college students. Generally, Ecstasy is taken through injection and rarely is snorted. This dangerous drug is produced in illegal laboratories and sold on the streets. When Ecstasy is taken with alcohol or other drugs, the users may be simultaneously addicted to more than one drug and suffer from adverse effects. Most of the Ecstasy pills sold in the streets are not pure. They often contain other toxic chemicals and recreational drugs, like PCP, heroin, crack, and even poison. As a result many Ecstasy users end up seeking first aid medical assistance. Ecstasy, like most recreational drugs, has a negative impact on the users' physical, psychoemotional, cognitive, and social world.

Physical Effects—Ecstasy causes the body's temperature and heart rate to increase dramatically, placing the user at high risk to have hyperthermia (heatstroke). Hyperthermia is considered as the number one cause of death among Ecstasy users. It also causes liver and kidney failure due to excessive dehydration. Ecstasy users have also reported blurred vision, nausea, chills, faintness, and muscle tension.

Psycho-emotional Effects—Ecstasy as well as MDA cause neurons to release a neurotransmitter known as serotonin. Seretonin, the brain chemical that many antidepressants (Prozac, Paxil, Effexor, Zoloft, Wellbutrin, and others) regulate, is responsible for the emotions and other processes. When Ecstasy enters the users' brain, it makes them feel temporarily relaxed, euphoric, peaceful, and loving. However, the extremely fast consumption of serotonin depletes the normal serotonin levels and produces depression, dysphoria, anxiety, insomnia, and poor appetite after the drug wears off. Individuals that are predisposed to depression are at risk to become chronically depressed if they use Ecstasy.

Cognitive Effects—Researchers have found that heavy Ecstasy users continue to experience difficulty in learning, retaining, and recalling information long after they withdrew from this toxic drug. This is related to the damage of the serotonin receptors that are unable to carry the messages to the brain. Brain images of chronic Ecstasy users show that when the serotonin-releasing parts of the cells are damaged by Ecstasy, some of the cells die, but others try to branch out. Unfortunately, they tend to grow in areas where they should not, and consequently they release serotonin in the wrong places of the brain. This affects learning and memory as much as the loss of serotonin itself. Ecstasy-using students are more likely to experience academic failure, truancy, and misconduct problems.

Social Effects—Ecstasy along with ketamine and GHB (gamma hydroxybuturate) are among the hallucinogen drugs that are heavily used in clubs and other dance parties by young adults and affect one's self-control. Being under the influence of a psychotropic drug and in the mist of a raving atmosphere, many of these Ecstasy and MDA users lose the sense of reality and expose themselves to high-risk behaviors. Self-delusional teens are often lured into promiscuous and unsafe sex, raping, kidnapping, use of alcohol and other toxic-laced drugs, and even death. According to the National Center on Addiction and Substance Abuse, fourteen-year-old teens are three times more likely to be offered Ecstasy and other illegal drugs now than in the past. By the time the adolescents reach age seventeen, 46 percent of them will attend a party where alcohol/drugs, including Ecstasy or prescription drugs, are used (CASA, 2006).

The evidence is overwhelming that Ecstasy is a

dangerous drug whose use continues to increase among adolescents and young adults. This urges parents/care-takers and all those that are involved in the lives of the children to engage in an immediate and effective manner to reduce young people's risk of experimenting or using Ecstasy and all other recreational drugs, because the price is too high. Our children's minds as well as their precious lives are at stake!

GHB (Gamma Hydroxybutyrate)

GHB, also known as a designer drug, is an odorless, colorless, and lightly salty-tasting drug. Generally, it is ingested in liquid form but at times in tablets or capsules. Prior to becoming a recreational drug, GHB was marked as an herbal supplement for insomnia and depression and also was used by bodybuilders for muscle enhancement. The effects of the drug begin within ten to twenty minutes after taking it, and its duration may be up to four hours. GHB is hard to be detected by medical tests because it leaves the body so fast. GHB is a powerful sedative drug, like ketamine and rohypnol, and even small doses may lead to loss of consciousness. It is also highly addictive and habitual, causing physical and psychological dependence even if it is used for a short period of time. There are some limited treatment programs for heavy GHB users; however, professionals claim that it is more difficult to seize the addiction of GHB than heroin or crack.

Effects of GHB—GHB is the most dangerous club

drug because of its immediate effects. It has caused seventy-three deaths since 1995, and the emergency admissions have quadrupled nationwide between 1998 to 2000, with an estimate of about 5,000 cases, and the use of the drug continues to grow (Brown University, 2004). Although researchers do not exactly know how this powerful drug affects the users' neurochemistry, evidence proposes that GHB acts in the brain directly and thus affects the physiological mechanism that controls the release of chemicals and nutrients to the brain.

Short-term research reported that GHB users experience disinhibition, enhanced sexual experiences and sociability, and increase of energy. Hallucinations, confusion, memory loss, anxiety, tremors, slow breathing and heart rate, and loss of consciousness are some of the symptoms of the GHB overdosed users. It has a negative impact on students' memory, learning, and their school responsibilities. Being preoccupied with the obsession of their GHB habit, they fail to complete their homework assignments, studying, and attending school. Consequently, they are held back or drop out of school and thus become easy prey of victimization by drug dealers and other dangerous individuals.

I recall one of my teen patients relating that he did not pass the eleventh grade due to excessive absenteeism. He used to miss school quite often because he could not sleep all night trying to figure out how he would find the money and the transportation to go to buy GHB and LSD the next day. Furthermore, he stated that school was too stressful for him and he would rather be out there doing his own thing. When I asked him why he used drugs knowing that they affected his education and his future, he replied, "Because they help me deal with the peer pressure and to make a lot of friends." It is heartbreaking to realize that our young children are misled by temporary pleasures, which threaten their lives and jeopardize their future for the mere fact that they have not been taught about the high risk of such harmful drugs. It is time for action and commitment to save our future generations from the sharp claws of recreational drugs that distort the vulnerable minds of our young people.

Ketamine

Ketamine is an injectable anesthetic commonly used by veterinarians and on the battlefields for surgery. Its recreational use began around 1980 and is sold as a dry white powder or clear liquid. The powder (the residue of the drying liquid) is crushed and snorted or smoked. Its effects are immediate and last approximately an hour. Ketamine is also a club drug and has become one of the fastest growing drugs among young people who prefer to take it over Ecstasy. Like Ecstasy and GHB, ketamine has divergent effects including stimulant, sedative, anesthetic, and hallucinogenic possessions. Ketamine makes the users feel euphoric, insensitive to physical pain, and distant from their surroundings, because it blocks the neurotransmitter "glutamate" at one of its receptors.

Effects of Ketamine—The anecdotal evidence from

the National Poisons Information Service indicates that ketamine intoxication cases have risen from ten in 1995 to more than 100 in 2001. The drug's effects are influenced by the weight of the users, tolerance, and presence of other drugs. Being a depressant, when ketamine is mixed with other drugs, such as alcohol, Valium, cocaine, heroin, etc., it reduces the heart rate and respiratory function and leads to death. Ketamine produces a wide range of effects in individuals. The drug is largely psychologically dependent causing hallucinations both visual and auditory. Muscle rigidity, violence, agitation, confusion, impairment in memory and learning are also associated with the use of this intoxicating drug. Its frequent use and high doses may alter the users' consciousness and induce neurosis as well as other mental illnesses. Ketamine has been recognized as one of the most powerful and psychedelic drugs, which is attractive to nightclub users and college students. It has also been identified as a high risk factor for "date rape" (Guardian, 2005). The reality is that our young people are surrounded by paramount and highly threatening enticements and our parental duty is to make them anti-drug/alcohol combatants.

Stimulants (known as Speed or Meth)

Methamphetamine is a powerful form of amphetamine, which comes in clear crystals or powder that can easily be dissolved in alcohol or water. It is also in re-crystallized form, known as Ice. This dangerous drug is widely produced in illegal laboratories with very highly toxic ingredients, such as battery acid, antifreeze, and drain cleaner. The user may snort, inject, swallow, or smoke the drug. Methamphetamine is used by all ages and sexes and vastly in the overpopulated areas and cities (National Institute on Drug Abuse, 2005).

Japanese were the first to synthesize methamphetamine and use it for reducing fatigue and enhancing productivity. In the 1960s methamphetamine was extremely popular, but because of its life threatening effects, its use declined. Unfortunately, this devastating drug reentered the alcohol and drug culture and seems to be increasingly popular among adults and teens. A 2004 NIDA-funded study reported that 5.2 percent of tenth graders and 6.2 percent of twelfth graders had tried this drug.

Effects of Methamphetamine—It is a stimulant drug that acts upon the central nervous system. Therapeutically, methamphetamine is used to produce elation, mental and health performance, extension of wakefulness, increase of activity, and curbing of appetite. This potent drug is highly addictive because it enters directly into the brain's *reward system*. This reward system is made up of a *neurocell net* (neurotransmitters), which works in synergy and helps humans and other living beings to do what is positive in order to preserve their existence. One particular drug that is responsible for the neurotransmitters' function is the neurochemical dopamine. As soon as Methamphetamine enters the mind, the reward system's neurotransmitters release excessive dopamine and work hard in order to absorb it.

The build up of dopamine in the brain causes feelings of euphoria and a sharp state of energy, which are registered in the reward system (U.S. Drug Enforcement Administration, 2006).

Recreational Methamphetamine, which tends to be frequently and heavily used, rapidly increases the production of dopamine and the activity of the brain. This decreases some of the brain's dopamine receptors damaging users' ability to feel pleasure humanly. Then the users need to highly increase the doses of dopamine in order to experience the same pleasure and inadvertently expose themselves to diverse physical and psychological risks. The physical and psychological risks of recreational methamphetamine and other stimulant drugs may cause cardiovascular complications, stroke, damage to small blood vessels in the brain, high blood pressure, increase the body's temperature, shortness of breath, gastrointestinal problems, even death. Heavy users may experience paranoia, mood disturbances, hallucinations, hostility, agitation, and suicidal or homicidal tendencies. Anxiety, confusion, violent and erratic behavior, and decrease of sexual function (especially in men) are also associated with heavy methamphetamine use. Tolerance may develop rapidly, and physical and psychological dependence may occur. Abrupt cessation, even if the drug is heavily used for a short period of time (two to three days), is usually followed by anxiety, depression, craving, and extreme fatigue. Overdose is also associated with high fever, convulsion, and heart attacks.

Although the degree of methamphetamine's use in

the U.S. is not certain, the number seeking medical care due to its hazardous effects is on the rise and places our youth at high risk. Stimulants should be of great concern to parents/caretakers and all those involved in the children's welfare because of their intricacy in their use as therapeutic and recreational or illicit drugs. The concepts on *stimulants* provided above are educational, reliable, empowering, and enlightening. I encourage readers to share this information with their young people as well as every teen that they come across who is caught in the increased popularity of the illicit stimulants.

Inhalants

Inhalants are chemical substances that fall into several categories, such as volatile solvents, gases, and volatile nitrites. Some examples of these categories are:

Solvents—Paint thinners, degreasers, dry cleaning fluids, spray lubrications, gasoline, kerosene, glues and adhesives, liquid lighter fluid, nail polish and remover, and furniture polish and wax products. School products, i.e., permanent felt tip markets, correction fluids, enamel paints, dry erase markers, and electronic contact cleaners.

Gases and Propellants—Gases/propellants used in butane lighters, propane, spray paints, hair and deodorant sprays, room deodorizer sprays, and refrigerants. Medical anesthetic gases, ether, chloroform, and halothane.

Volatile Nitrites—Aliphatic nitrites including amyl,

butyl, and isobutyl, which are sold over-the-counter as deodorizers and liquid incense under the brand names of Rush, Bolt, and Locker Room.

Inhalants may be snorted, huffed, or bagged to produce intoxicating effects, like alcohol. They are highly used by children between ages ten to twelve because they can easily be accessed, are low cost, and are legal. According to the Substance Abuse and Mental Health Administration's 2001 National Household Survey on Drug Abuse, approximately two million young people ages twelve to seventeen have used an inhalant in the last year. Another survey in 2003 reported that 23 million (9.7%) persons ages twelve and older have used an inhalant once in their lifetime. Unfortunately, most of us are not aware of the high prevalence of inhalants among our young children and that their delirious effects may lead to a fatal episode from the first time experimentation or use. I believe that inhalants should be included in our educational agenda when we discuss alcohol, marijuana, and all other recreational drugs with our inquisitive children.

How Inhalants Affect the User—Inhalants affect both the body and the mind because they damage the fatty tissues (myelin) that cover the nerve cells (neurotransmitters). When the myelin breaks down, the nerve cells may not be able to transmit messages to the nervous system and the brain. Some inhalants depress the central nervous system, which causes decreased respiration and blood pressure. Others increase the size of blood vessels, allowing more blood to flow through, thus causing damage in the heart, kidneys, liver, and adrenal gland (Mind Over Matter, 1998, 2002).

Consequences—Almost all inhalants have similar effects as anesthetics, but their potential consequences depend on the inhalants' chemical properties and doses. The user may feel stimulation, less inhibition, loss of consciousness, and even *sudden sniffing death syndrome*. Additional possible effects related to inhalants' uses are: headaches, nausea, slurred speech, and loss of motor coordination. Mental effects may include fear, anxiety, depression, unpredictable behavior, memory impairment, attention deficits, and diminished non-verbal intelligence with chronic users. Furthermore, inhalants' harmful effect on pregnant women is similar to Fetal Alcohol Syndrome.

Studies have shown that as alcohol and recreational drugs affect the abusers' families and schools; inhalants also affect the users' social constitution. The homeostasis of their family is threatened due to poor relationships between the young users, parents, and siblings; their scholastic performance and conformity to school policies are challenged, and the rate of dropout from school increases. Chronic inhalers often have a history of violence and delinquent activities that disrupt community productivity and generate financial burden. Inhalant users tend to become social outcasts mainly gravitating to other inhalant users (National Inhalant Prevention Coalition, 2006). Lack of supervision, inconsistency in family life, peer pressure, easy availability, and low cost of inhalants are some of the existing reasons that children and teens become involved with these deadly drugs.

Given the above facts, we should not underestimate the high risk of the harmful inhalants that invade our children's bodies and minds at a very young age. Therefore, our educational mission to make them know their hazardous consequences should start as early as possible.

Anabolic Steroids

Steroids are hormonal substances that are chemically and pharmacologically related to testosterone that promotes muscle growth. Therapeutically, anabolic steroids are used for certain types of anemia and for males that produce inadequate levels of testosterone. They are also used for treating animals' damaged tissues due to illness and trauma.

Unfortunately, many young individuals use anabolic steroids for building muscles, and they illegally buy them in the black market. In 1991 the U.S. Congress placed anabolic steroids as a class of drugs into Schedule III of the Controlled Substance Act (Drugs of Abuse Publication, 2006). Various reports indicate that anabolic steroids' use has increased significantly among adolescents. The 2003 Monitoring the Future Study revealed 2.5 percent of eighth graders, 3 percent of tenth graders and 3.5 percent of twelfth graders have used steroids at least once in their lifetime. Steroids may be taken in the form of pills or injected directly into muscles. Abusers take doses 10 to 100 times more than a medical prescription allows. Some users tend to take two different kinds of steroids simultaneously for faster results. This is called *stacking*. Others start with low doses and slowly increase into higher doses. This is called *pyramid* and may last six to twelve weeks. Neither of these approaches lead to favorable results.

Effects of Steroids—There are high risks associated with the use of steroids. When they enter the body, they reach different organs and muscles and cause their cells to produce excessive proteins that form malignant tumors. Medical studies show that steroids cause cardiovascular and liver damage, cerebrovascular toxicity, elevated blood pressure, and cholesterol. They also have disfiguring effects on both girls and boys (i.e. severe acne, premature hair receding, and greasy hair). Young athletes who abuse steroids have died from heart attack due to the *arteriosclerosis*, which causes fat deposits inside the arteries (National Institute on Drug Abuse, 2000).

Male steroid users experience enlargement of breast, knows as *gynecomastia*, while females develop muscular characteristics, such as deepening voice, breast size decrease, irregular menstruation, and reduced sexual functioning. Studies also show that steroid abusers may have psychotic reactions, manic episodes, aggression, hostility, and violent behaviors (National Institute on Drugs abuse for Teens, 2006). It is scientifically proven that steroids are very dangerous drugs and indeed present a high risk in our young people and especially to our athletes who strive for physical perfection and athletic success.

In this chapter I described in a credible manner the most prevalent drugs that attract our young people today. I hope the presenting information becomes a reliable teaching resource for all readers. The forthcoming chapter, a vivid revealing of the paramount etiologies that make young people to succumb to chemical substance abuse, will empower your commitment to the prevention of alcohol and drug use that threatens every child.

Chapter 3

What Causes Young People to Succumb to Alcohol and Other Drugs

Reach deep into my inquisitive mind
Teach me the art of thinking
Reasoning and strive and
I pledge never to fail you
Parents of mine.

—Anthony N. Betances,
Recognized National Poet

Sociologists, psychologist and other experts who have studied the alcohol/drug subculture support that the reasons young people use alcohol/drugs are multi-dimensional and profound. This chapter will discuss three eminent variables that are proven to be associated with alcohol and drug use/abuse, known as *esoteric, exoteric,* and *circumstantial* variables.

Esoteric variables refer to genetic predisposition and psycho-synthesis (psychological make up) of the individual.

Exoteric variables are related to an individual's environment—family, peers, school, and societal influences.

Circumstantial variables are an individual's exposure to terrorism, wars, earthquakes, and other natural disasters.

Esoteric Variables

Genetic predisposition to alcohol use/abuse has been extensively researched and found to be highly linked to genes (see Chapter 1 for detailed explanation). Researchers through the study of pedigrees of large families with addiction can identify if a trait has a genetic component. This means whether or not this trait is passed from parent to child through the genes. This phenomenon is very significant and highly predisposes a child to alcoholism and other drugs. There is great evidence that children born to an alcoholic parent, even when raised by non-alcoholic adopted parents, have a much higher rate of becoming alcoholic than those with non-alcoholic origin. For example, the Texas University's Addiction Science Research and Education Center found that more than 60 percent of alcoholics have a family history of alcoholism. In addition, children of alcoholic parents have an early onset and are two to four times more likely to become alcoholics or addicts. Latest research also reveals evidence of biological vulnerability to other drug abuse. Children of heroin parents are more likely found to be heroin addicts (Kaufman, 1988). Scientists hope within five to ten years, through the use of advanced imaging technologies, to be able to identify neurochemical activity in the brain that contributes to drug use/abuse. However, because drug addiction is influenced by multiple genetic factors, what scientists really search for are the *biological and hormonal* factors that make some people susceptible to addiction and not others. But, there are still great individual differences in the neural structure of the brain and the production of hormones that make some individuals vulnerable to develop a chemical substance disorder and not others. Psychological and biological researchers have identified temperamental traits that are vulnerable factors to chemical substance use/abuse. According to H.J. Eysenck & M.W. Eysenck's personality model, some of these traits may be *extraversion*, *neuroticism*, and *psychoticism*.

Extraverted individuals are chronically under-aroused and bored. They are therefore in need of external stimulation in order to reach an optimal level of performance. This causes a high impulsivity, which is empirically related to substance use. Children, who were diagnosed at age three with high levels of restlessness and impulsivity, tend to be diagnosed with alcohol dependency and other drug use in adolescence.

Neurotic people experience high levels of emotional

reactivity to events and high levels of anxiety and anger because they have low activation thresholds when faced with relatively minor stressors. Therefore, neurotic personalities experience high internal distress, and they often drink or use recreational drugs to medicate themselves. Aggressiveness in children, as young as age five to ten years old, was also found to predict adolescence's use/abuse of alcohol and other drugs. However, hostility was associated with binge drinking in high school children, but not during young adulthood.

Psychoticism is characterized by thought-mindedness, non-conformity, hostility, and impulsivity; underlying personality traits that have been posited to be risk factors for substance use/abuse. It is persuasive that extraversion, neuroticism, and psychoticism predispose individuals to initiation and continuation of substance use and abuse (Measurement of Impulsivity in a Hierarchical Model of Personality Traits: Implication for Substance Use, 2006).

I concur that personality traits are significantly alarming for the onset of alcohol and drugs, especially among the adolescents. I found that most of my young patients possess one of the above personalities (extraversion, neuroticism, or psychoticism), and whether or not are genetically predisposed to chemical substance, they are more gregarious than the inhibited adolescents (stable introverts) to enter the alcohol/drug culture. In addition, it is noticed that the extroverts tend to have higher levels of impulsivity and anxiety.

Lately, research focuses on the relationship between mental illness and substance abuse because of the increased number of individuals suffering from both conditions. Experts estimate that approximately 60 percent of people with one of these pathologies are fighting both. Dr. Alan Manevitz, a psychiatrist of New York Hospital, in New York, states that mental health problems and substance abuse, known as comorbidity, seem to appear together because one is more vulnerable to the other. Chemical substance use often *triggers* the onset of mental problems, whether or not there is a biological or genetic predisposition.

Some of these psychiatric substance induced conditions are mood and psychotic disorders, anxiety disorders, sexual dysfunctions, and sleep disorders. Their substance-induced agents are alcohol and sedatives, amphetamines and cocaine, hallucinogens and phencyclidine, inhalants and opioids and cannabis for anxiety disorders (DSM-IV, 1994). Individuals with psychiatric disorders (i.e., anxiety, affective disorders, schizophrenia, and other disorders) tend to abuse chemical substances two to five times more in order to relieve their painful emotions. Examples of such selective self-medications may be stimulants for augmentation of depression, low self-esteem, hypomania, hyperactivity, and opiates for aggression, rage, and disorganization; alcohol and CNS depressants for closeness, dependency, and self-assertion (Khantzian, 1990). It is worthy of notice that among the mental illnesses that have captured the interest of latest research is *bipolar disorder*. This is an illness characterized by cycles of extreme mood swings or episodes. These episodes can take three forms: deep depression, elation, or mania. Individuals that suffer from bipolar disorder, particularly females, have a high rate of alcoholism, approximately seven times more than the universal population (Boucher, 2006). Substance-induced psychiatric disorders are very difficult to treat and substance abuse/dependency should be first addressed before any other treatment is implemented.

Exoteric Variables

Among the major exoteric factors are family, peer pressure, personal expectations and school and societal influences. These variables have been well researched and proven to play a critical role in the adolescents' alcohol drug use/abuse.

Family—According to U.S. Department of Health and Human Services and SAMHSA's (Substance Abuse and Mental Health Services Administration) National Clearinghouse for Alcohol and Drug Information, there are an estimated 26.8 million children of alcoholics in the United Sates. Preliminary research suggests that over 11 million are under the age of eighteen. Research on alcoholism and family influence supports that parallel to genetic predisposition, parental favorable attitudes about drinking and modeling have also been associated with adolescent's initiating and continuing drinking. It is not amazing that children whose parents drink or use illegal drugs are more likely to follow in their parents' footsteps.

Absenteeism of a parent, due to death or incarceration (in 1999, 1.5 million minor children had a parent in prison), lack of parental supervision and monitoring, lack of family interaction and communication between parents, and children and family conflict have been significantly linked to early alcohol use onset among adolescents, chronic and severe alcohol use, and the likely manifestation of additional problematic behaviors. Inconsistent parental direction or discipline, unusual permissiveness, or severe discipline, constant criticism and the absence of parental recognition and praise are also associated with high rates of alcohol and drug use among adolescents. In addition, many of these emotionally neglected youths tend to run away from home, become members of gangs and excessively use illicit drugs or prescription-type drugs. In 2002, approximately 1.6 million youths, ages twelve to seventeen, ran away from home. Approximately 50 percent of them used alcohol and 23.2 percent used illicit drugs other than marijuana (National Survey on Drug Use and Health, 2004). Children that are raised in alcohol/drug environments tend to experience feelings of loneliness, isolation, poor-self-esteem, shame, and anxiety. They experience problems in expressing themselves in social interactions, intimate relationships, and later on in work performance. In order to escape their pain, they often seek relief through self-medication and consequently use alcohol/drugs earlier than those children that do not live in alcohol/drug environments.

Research also supports that an alcoholic family environment may affect a child's IQ test scores. I highly recognize the validity to these findings. Being a school psychologist for five years and having tested over 500 hundred students, I have found approximately 20 percent of those students that come from alcohol/drug environments function at a low average cognitive level. Furthermore, they experience emotional problems, such as Attention Deficit-Hyperactivity Disorder, anxiety, depression, social withdrawal and conduct problems. Given the above facts, it is evident that the dynamics of the family play a leading role in the adolescence and young adults' direction in life.

Peer Influence—A peer is an individual with whom a child identifies, generally, but not always, from the same age group. Peer influence occurs when the individual or individuals experience implicit or overt persuasion to accept the similar beliefs, values or expectation and goals as those of his/her peers.

During adolescence, peers play a large part in adolescents' life and often replace family in their social and leisure involvements. Some theorists and researchers argue that an unsupportive family environment, which generates feelings of alienation and despair, often encourages young people to join peer groups that use alcohol/drugs. Most of these individuals fail to recognize the seriousness of their risky decision. In consequence, the lack of mature judgment and the sense of responsibility draw these defenseless adolescents to their peers' perilous style of life, *use of alcohol/drugs*. Peer conformity, which is considered an important prerequisite for social acceptance, might also be another factor that lures young individuals to alcohol/drug use. Researchers and substance abuse therapists report that many adolescents have become victims of heavy drinking, drug use and other antisocial behaviors by compromising their values and beliefs and succumbing to peer pressure.

Personal Expectancy—Another variable that has been recognized as an influential factor for alcohol and drug use/abuse is the adolescents' personal *expectancy* (expectancy is a cognitive schema—an acquired relationship between a stimulus and a response). The alcohol/drug expectancy memory system is part of the contributory pathway leading to their use and abuse. For example an adolescent seeks out alcohol/drugs or engages in a risk behavior in order to obtain desired gratification. There is substantial evidence that expectancies adjudicate addictive behavioral outcomes. Expectancies appear in children before actual chemical substance use/abuse begins and prospectively predicts chemical substance use. Before children enter adolescence, they have already formed their outcome expectancies about smoking, drinking, and other substances, often associated with positive or negative outcomes. Some of these expectances may be formed through modeling or media portrayals. However, when children engage in actual alcohol/drug use, their expectancies change from primarily negative (unpleasant outcomes) to positive social effects, mood, and arousal. These expectancies are the ones that predict future alcohol/drug use and abuse, or other risky behaviors and they should be altered through education, motivation, and exposure to positive styles of life (Miller, Smith & Goldman, 1990).

School—Children that are poor achievers in school tend to enter the alcohol and drug culture earlier than their counterparts who are successful. Boredom and disinterest in schoolwork also appear to drive young people into drug use and abuse. Non-participation in extra curricular activities, i.e. sports, student council, chorus, band, multi-cultural and science clubs, or youth and religious programs increase the change of substance use/abuse involvement. Frequent truancy, cutting classes, suspensions, and expulsions give the youth excess unstructured time that may be an attractive temptation to the potential association with drug/alcohol users and activities (American Council for Drug and Education's Web Site, 2006).

Societal Influences—Children that are in conflict with the community where they live and feel alienated from the dominant social values of authority are more likely to use alcohol/drugs than those that adhere to the norms. These confused children are often turned off by society and do not care for themselves or anyone else. Consequently, they lose perspective of the future and seek gratification for the present through the use of alcohol and drugs. Rebellious children that lack social responsibility and exhibit early antisocial behaviors, such as aggression, violence, and other delinquent behaviors, are also prognostic for early alcohol/drug onset and abuse.

Children today live in an era that allows them to be exposed to a drug subculture world through *television, newspapers, radio, shows,* and *conversations* from a very young age. Being in a state of learning, children's inquisitive minds process and restore this glamorized information in their learning repertoire, not recognizing the harm and risk. During adolescence, these memories and learned behaviors will have a strong influence on teens' attitudes toward alcohol/drug choices (Child Development Institute, 2006). Studies have found that mass media is an important means for adolescents to learn about drugs, and they perceive them as a trusted and influential source of information. Considering the fact that an average child watches approximately ten to sixteen hours weekly *general*-audience programs, it is unlikely that children would escape the viewing of movies, shows, music, and advertisements, which convey overt or veiled chemical substance use messages. For example, alcohol is usually presented as a *social* drink with generally positive consequences. It is a universal phenomenon that every celebration on TV is inaugurated with alcohol served regardless of children's presence. Conversely, although marijuana is rarely portrayed, it is regarded by most teens and even by many adults as a harmless drug, which is hardly ever associated with serious consequences. Studies have also revealed that 98 percent of the twenty most popular movies rented by teens during 1996 and 1997 *depict* use of at least one chemical substance. In addition, 27 percent out of the 1,000 most popular *music recordings* from these two years *contained a lucid reference of either alcohol or illicit drugs* (Holland, 1999). Alcohol in rap song lyrics is more likely to promote positive than negative results and consequences. These findings tend to be consistent with the recognized aspect that rap music has been profoundly affected by the marketing of alcoholic beverages, which happened to be used by many young individuals (Herd, D, 2005).

The availability and easy accessibility of drugs, especially with the increase of production of *designer drugs* (i.e., methamphetamine, Ecstasy, LSD, methcathinone or CAT, etc.) in the United States, threaten the lives of many young children and allures teens to become early participants in the drug culture. A large amount of these drugs are manufactured in underground laboratories and homes and sold on the streets. For example, methamphetamine (MA), the most addictive drug among all designers' drugs, whose production has dramatically increased across the nation, was found to be manufactured in the homes of abused children. The reported number of children present at *MA laboratory busts* across the nation increased from 950 in 1999 to over 3,300 in 2002 (Counselor, The Magazine for Addiction Professionals, 2005). These findings are disturbing because they have a twofold consequence. First, the children are exposed to a uniquely dangerous and damaging environment because of the drugs' toxic effects, and second, the innocent children learn from their parents that drug use is a normal and validated behavior. Although the propensity for alcohol sales to youth appears to be reduced, we still find a large number of establishments, especially in impoverished or affluent areas, to break the drinking *under age law* and pursue their illegal alcohol sales. I had the opportunity to treat many young individuals (between ages sixteen and eighteen), who were on probation for DUI violations or school suspensions. In their own admission, they did not have any difficulty purchasing alcohol from their neighborhood liquor stores or having their older brothers or older friends buy it for them. In addition, being self-absorbed and unwilling to believe that their family's money could not solve their minor problem (as they often referred to drinking) found themselves to be in trouble with the law. On the other hand, a respectful portion of my low-income counselees confessed that they would not have used alcohol and drugs if they were residing in neighborhoods where visible drug sales and visibly intoxicated people were not present.

Another troubling factor that has received special attention by social researchers is the relation of *poverty* to chemical substance abuse/use. Poverty is a salient social problem that affects all racial and ethnic populations as well as our vulnerable youth. A 2001 survey conducted by the National Public Radio (NPR), the Kaiser Family Foundation, and Harvard University's Kennedy School of Government found that drug abuse is prevalent practice among the poor. Poverty indeed is a serious concern among Americans, who believe that it is related to many etiologies. For example, lack of jobs or low wages, single parent families, illnesses, declining of moral values, incarceration, homelessness, and chemical substance abuse. Astonishingly, even low income Americans, those living below the federal poverty level, viewed *drug abuse* as a characteristic of poverty. This implies that impoverished individuals are more likely to abuse chemical substances than their counterparts.

Research conducted for the San Francisco home-

less population found that 70 percent of them had substance abuse problems and 30–40 percent suffered from
medical fragility and mental illness (Tuprin and Tate,
1997). Many homeless adolescents lacking a parental
figure are easily gravitated to locations where they are
most likely introduced to drug use and other antisocial
behaviors and activities (Kurtz et al., 1991). For example, survival sex and trade of sex for money or drugs is
a fearsome problem among the homeless adolescents
that are often banned from welfare hotels and live on
the streets. According to Whitebeck and Hoyt's (2002)
four years study of homeless adolescents, sex trading
for drugs seems to be a more daunting problem among
runway adolescent females than boys. They also investi-
gated the negative developmental effects of early sexual
abuse on runaway adolescents and concluded that this
places them at high risk for sexual activity and early
drug abuse.

Although poverty is not a separate gender issue, it
appears to place poor young females in a more defenseless arena. The consequences of being poor may be
extremely high ranging from early chemical substance
abuse to transmitted deadly diseases and frequently to
sexual slavery. Motherhood, poverty, and drug abuse
are on the rise among teenagers in the inner cities
whose families are already on welfare and overwhelmed
with physical or mental problems (Waters, J., Roberts,
A.R. & Morgen, K., 1997). On the other hand, many
of young male youths, who are caught in the web of
poverty, parallel to use/abuse drugs, join street and out-
law motorcycle gangs and become active participants in

the trafficking and smuggling of drugs, such as heroin, cocaine/crack, methamphetamines, etc. A high percentage of these juveniles end up in jails or detention centers where they often acquire more serious and destructive behaviors. Thus, when they are mainstreamed back into society, they do not hesitate to engage in somber illegal acts or crimes that may lead them to death or to loss of their personal freedom, not to mention the astronomically large financial burden imposed on our society. It is evident that poverty plays an important role in the upsurge in teenage drug use together with the plethora of other potential factors.

Circumstantial Variables

Circumstantial factors refer to catastrophic events that are associated with an individual or individuals' exposure to terrorism, wars, earthquakes, and other natural disasters. Researchers have long recognized the powerful impact of these factors on altering human behavior and changing the course of life. Due to the wide spectrum of the circumstantial factors, we will discuss some of the catastrophic events that have received great attention because they place people at a high risk for alcohol and drug use/abuse and relapse.

Individuals that are directly or indirectly involved in these devastating situations experience a magnitude of stress reactions, known as post-traumatic stress disorders (PTSD). Examples of these emotional manifestations are anxiety, depression, and substance use/abuse and addiction. Although exposure to stress is a common occurrence in the lives of many people across all ages, it is also one of the most influential factors for substance abuse and addiction, following direct or indirect exposure to a severe traumatic event(s).

Epidemiological studies reveal that children exposed to severe stress, such as parental loss, child abuse, terrorist attacks, and earthquake and hurricane experiences tend to demonstrate a strong relationship between psychosocial stressors in their early life and substance abuse in their adulthood. The following scientific explanations give us a better understanding of how stress works psychologically and biologically on the victims. A high complex network system, consisting by the central nervous, endocrine and immune and cardiovascular systems, mediates stress response. Stress activates adaptive responses (i.e., anxiety, fear, threat, etc.), and it releases the neurotransmitter norepinephrine, which is involved in memory. This is one of the reasons that people exposed to stressful events tend to remember more clearly and intensively these harmful situations than their counterparts. Stress is also responsible for the release of a hormone known in the scientific field as the corticotropin-releasing factor (CRF). This hormone initiates the responses to stress-stimuli, is found throughout the brain, and appears to increase its levels in high-risk situations. Amusingly, it has also been found that alcohol and all abused drugs increase the level of the corticotropin release hormone (NIDA Community Drug Alert Bulleting, 2002). Thus, this suggests a neurobiological association with stress and chemical substance abuse.

Emerging research of comorbid disorders has found that in many cases chemical substance use begins after the exposure to traumatic events and the development of PTSD, thus making PTSD a risk factor for drug abuse. A national research study following the September 11, 2001, terrorist attack in the United States revealed higher prevalence of PTSD to individuals closer to the disaster and those actually in the building or injured. Although prevalence of PTSD decreased during the six months after the disaster, alcohol and substance use remained high. Furthermore, depression was increased related to alcohol, cigarette, and marijuana use (Vlahov et al., 2002).

Another research study related to the Oklahoma City bombing, one year after the tragic event, reported increased rates of alcohol use, smoking, stress and PTSD symptoms as compared to citizens of other metropolitan cities (Smith et al., 1999). A study was conducted with sixty-one Vietnam combat veterans with post-traumatic stress disorder and alcohol/drug use and abuse. Its findings indicated that the onset of alcohol and chemical substance abuse was classically associated with the onset symptoms of PTSD. The natural course of alcohol and substance abuse parallels that of PTSD. That implies that as the PTSD patients' symptoms increased, the propensity for alcohol, marijuana, heroin, as well as benzodiazepines increased. (Bremner et al., 1996). In 2003, the National Research Center for Medical Sciences of Iran interviewed more than 160 people in the city of Bam during the first two weeks after a devastating earthquake. It was reported that opium abuse, which had been high among the male population, became a serious problem in the city. More than one third of the interviewers reported that they had used opium on the first day and two thirds during the second day to the end of the second week after the earthquake. About half of them received morphine or other analgesics from medical professionals (Movaghar et al., 2003). Keep in mind that stress related to catastrophic experiences affects people's brains, minds, and bodies in an orchestrated whole-organism response. Consequently, people are highly triggered to use/abuse alcohol and drugs, or relapse if they are in recovery. In an effort to escape their agonizing psychological and emotional pain, they frequently self-medicate.

I hope the above information increases the awareness and knowledge of the reader to recognize the high correlation between catastrophic events, stress, and chemical substance use/abuse. Furthermore, I hope it is apparent how harmful and damaging it would be for young children and teens to be exposed to such dramatic situations whose primitive defense mechanisms lacking healthy and productive strategies to cope with stressful events. Through teaching and modeling, your children and teens can gain healthy defenses that will assist them in dealing with the aftermath of painful memories of situations and events, which generate post-traumatic stress disorder, a proven factor of chemical substance use.

Chapter 4

Adolescence Chemical Substance Abuse Dependency and Treatment

> When I was a child your tender
> Touch healed my wound
> Every time
> Now that my wounds are deep
> And threaten my life
> Please don't abandon me
> I'm still your child...
>
> —Anthony Nicholas Betances,
> Recognized National Poet

Chemical Substance Abuse and Dependency

Substance abuse is defined as a chronic or habitual use of any chemical for the sake of its non-therapeutic effects on the mind or body, especially drugs or alcohol (Drug Addiction and Drug Abuse, Abadinsky, S., 1989). A habitual behavior can lead the user to a psychological and often physical state (dependency) characterized by a compulsion to use alcohol or drugs to maintain a feeling of contentment. Some researchers support that the definition of drug abuse and dependency is biased and infused with the political and moral values of a culture and society. For example, there are drinks (i.e., coffee and tea) that contain stimulant agents (caffeine) that are used by millions of people around the world. However, because of their moderately mild stimulatory consequences and non-triggering antisocial behaviors (in the users), they are not generally considered abused substances. Even narcotics' dependency is viewed only as drug abuse in certain social environments. In India, opium has been used for centuries without becoming excessively acidic to society.

The United States has the highest substance abuse rate of any industrialized nation. Government statistics (1997) show that 36 percent of the United States population has tried marijuana, cocaine, or other elicited drugs. By comparison, 71 percent of the population has smoked cigarettes, and 82 percent has tried alcoholic beverages. Marijuana is the most commonly used illicit drug. In 2005, the Monitoring the Future national survey results indicated that half of the students in the United States have tried an illegal drug before they graduated from high school. Most of the teens that used alcohol, cigarettes and marijuana engaged in this behavior before they reached age fourteen. What is more alarming is the teens' continued increase of non-medical use of prescription medications. Some of these medications are OxyContin, Vicodin, and sedatives/barbiturates. These drugs are powerful medicines and can be extremely dangerous in our teens' lives. As we all are aware, adolescence is a period during which youth tends to reject traditional authority figures in an effort to gain their independence. That may be a significant reason that a large number of teens engage in various risky behaviors, including alcohol and drugs.

Adolescents involved in substance abuse are also inclined to experience high incidents of psychopathology. For instance, 7 percent of a community sample of non-treatment-seeking adolescents received a DSM-III-R diagnosis of an alcohol or other substance use disorder. Ninety percent of the 7 percent were also diagnosed with a comorbid disorder, i.e., anxiety, depression, conduct disorder or post-traumatic stress disorder (Keller et al., 1992). Research also indicates that early use of alcohol and other substances may have a risky impact on successful developmental transitions. Transitions are *the paths that connect us to transformed physical, mental, and social selves* (Schulenburg et. al., 1997). Puberty, moving from high school to college, from school to work, and from being single to becoming married are some of the major transitions in one's life. These and other subtle transitions—for example, changes in relationships with parents, peers, romantic partners, changes in self-definition, and increased self-regulation—provide the structure which transforms children into adolescents and adolescents into young adults. It is obvious that the transitions to adulthood years are characterized with more and more diverse options, opportunities, and restraints. Thus, behavioral choices may greatly influence these transitions. For example, adolescents who do not follow normative paths and use alcohol/drugs may engage in early sexual activities, drop out of school, prematurely leave parents/caretakers' houses, and consequently face lower adulthood work-related status.

Etiological Factors of Substance Abuse

Researchers and practitioners agree that there are many etiologies that embed adolescents into alcohol and drug abuse. In this chapter, I will discuss three dominant factors that have been extensively researched: *psychiatric disorders, childhood sexual abuse,* and *childhood behavioral* problems. Genetics, family dynamics, and peer influence, which are considered as equally influential factors in the vulnerability of young individuals to alcohol/drug use and abuse, were already discussed in chapter 3.

Psychiatric Disorders—According to the American Academy of Pediatrics, adolescents who reported higher levels of drinking were more likely to have conduct disorder. In a study of adolescents in residential treatment for alcohol and illicit drug dependence, 25 percent met the DSM-II criteria for depression, three times the rate reported for controls. In 43 percent of these cases, the onset of alcohol and/or illicit drug dependence preceded the depression, in 35 percent the depression occurred first, and in 22 percent the disorder occurred simultaneous with depression. Alcohol abuse or dependence was also found to be twice as high among those with anxiety disorder (National Institute on Alcohol Abuse and Alcoholism, Youth Drinking: Risk Factor and Consequences, 1997). In another study of college students, the alcohol abusers were diagnosed to have four times more a major depressive disorder than those without alcohol abuse.

Childhood Sexual Abuse—Sexual abuse at a young age has been a predicator for the onset of early alcohol and drug/use and initiation of injection drug. Approximately 2143 young adult injection drug users were studied in five U.S. cities during 1997–1999. The proportion of young adults who had experienced sexual abuse (14.3%) was higher than that of the general population (8.5%). Furthermore, 72 percent of the sexually abused individuals have been abused before the initiation of injection drug use. It has been postulated from previous studies that childhood sexual abuse leads to depression, substance abuse, re-victimization and other internalizing and externalizing behaviors. Exposure to these paramount stressors in early life may be the mechanism through which early substance abuse and early injection drug use happens (Ompad, D.C. et al., 1997–1999). Obviously, childhood sexual abuse can be considered a high risk for chemical substance abuse in our children. This warrants an integrating substance abuse and post victimization treatment in order to protect the health of young adults.

Childhood Behavior Problems—Researchers have

associated childhood certain behaviors as predictors of alcohol and other drug use in adolescence. Children that were diagnosed at age three with high levels of restlessness and impulsivity tend to be diagnosed with alcohol dependency and other drug use in adolescence. Aggressiveness in children, ages five to ten, was also found to predict adolescents' alcohol and other drug use. However, hostility was associated with binge drinking in high school children, but not during young adulthood.

According to Dr. Robert A. Zucker of the National Institute of Health on Alcohol Abuse and Alcoholism, sleep problems in early childhood appear to pre-dict alcohol and drugs use/abuse during adolescence. Approximately 257 boys were studied with *sleep distur-bance* during their toddler years. The results showed that they were 2.3 times more likely to have started using alcohol by age fourteen, 2.3 times more likely to smoke cigarettes, and 2.6 times more likely to use marijuana than the boys that did not have any sleeping problems. The researched sample did not include any subjects with genetic predisposition to alcoholism. Although early childhood sleep problems predicted attention and anxiety/depression in late childhood, these prob-lems did not predict the onset of substance abuse inde-pendent of sleep problems. The medical researchers proposed three possible reasons for this phenomenon. First, sleep problems and substance problems may share some neurobiological dysfunction, which has not yet been clearly identified. Second, lack of sleep may lead to poor choices and judgment in peer selections and activity involvement. Third, problematic sleep teens may use drugs to self-medicate in order to relieve their emotional and physical distress. These findings should be alarming to those parents that observe their children experiencing insomnia and overtiredness and should consult their children's health professionals.

Treatment

Epidemiological and treatment research on adolescent alcohol and substance abuse has shown that the earlier the age of alcohol use onset and the more chronic and severe the course of alcohol use is, the more likely the manifestation of multi-dimensional problems becomes. Antisocial behaviors, mental health disorders, traumatic stress syndrome, and social dysfunction in school and family are among the most serious tribulations that dominate the life of those audacious adolescents. Therefore, the appropriate theoretical matrix for developing efficacious treatment of adolescent alcohol/drug abuse disorders will be one that seeks to explain and beneficially influence multiple biological and social dimensions. Such treatment will mediate and moderate adolescent health, behavior, and social function.

In general, adolescents do not identify themselves as problem drinkers or drug users. An optimal approach to this is to develop proactive screening, assessment, and treatment procedures that target settings in which adolescents with these problems are likely to present. Urgent care settings, primary care clinics, and courts are

potentially good intention sites. School-based prevention programs have been somewhat effective, but they
are unable to reach out and motivate those adolescents
that are already heavily involved in the abuse of alcohol
and other drugs.

Among the various interventions implemented for
adolescents and young adults' alcohol/drug abuse is the
Motivational Enhancement Intervention (MI), known
also as brief therapy. This approach is widely used and
is promising for emergency room (ER) settings and
perhaps other settings in which there is the potential
for a teachable moment. MI is particularly effective in
reducing harmful behaviors, for example, traffic violations among older adolescents and drunkenness and
driving among younger adolescents (Monti, P. et. al.,
2001, Chapter 5).

In order to enhance the adolescent's interest in brief
treatment, *personalized feedback* from the assessment
instruments is provided. This includes a comparison of
the teen's scores to age and gender norms on drinking
frequency and quantity, drunkenness, alcohol-related
problems with family, school and peers, physical and
emotional dependence (including signs of tolerance
and withdrawal), and risk taking. In addition, the teens
are informed about their blood alcohol level results at
the time they are treated at the hospital. Motivation
can also be further enhanced by probing the teens to
envision the future as alcohol users and not users. An
example of a prompt might be, *If you decided to make
a change, what do you think would become easier in your
athletic/school aspirations or future life?* The intent of

this approach is to persuade teens to consider the further potential negative outcome of continuing drinking and encourage them to accept a change for positive outcomes.

The MI therapy also allows the adolescents to discuss and contemplate with the counselor a plan of commitment to giving up drinking and drugs during therapy and after discharge. This will definitely help the adolescents to be more successful with their treatment, especially if their self-efficacy is previously enhanced. Thus, the adolescents will not only be willing to change, but they will also become confident that they can be successful. Such plans must include short and long term reasonable and attainable goals, as well as effective strategies that will help the adolescent to handle barriers, challenging situations. The MI plan tends to be more effective if the goals are personalized, concrete, behavioral, and the plan includes a timetable. Furthermore, it is highly effective if delivered by well-trained counselors, who are experienced in therapy skills and behavioral principles.

Another foremost therapy, which has widely been recognized by substance abuse researchers and therapists, is the *Integrative Behavioral and Family Therapy* (IBFT). This model combines two treatment approaches for adolescent substance abuse, family therapy, and individual cognitive-behavioral therapy. It is an outpatient therapeutic program, predominantly intense, which is office-based and lasts around ten to sixteen sessions (Waldron, H. et al. 2001, Chapter 7). The major goals of the IBFT intervention are to (a) reduce or eliminate substance use and other problematic behaviors and to (b) improve family relationships.

Personally, I favor the *Integrative Behavioral and Family Therapy* (IBFT) and frequently utilize it with my teens, who find it enjoyable because it allows them to interact with the therapist. Through role-playing, I teach my patients: *how to cope with cravings, how to solve problems through communication skills, and how to manage their anger, depression, and other negative moods.* The mastering of the above skills is an integral part of my patients' therapy, and I consider them as critical prerequisites for chemical substance refusal.

Craving—It is a sudden impulse that drives an individual to engage in an act, such as drinking or using drugs. Craving is the subjective desire to experience the effects of consequences of such an act (Marltatt & Gorden, 1985). In order to control the cravings of my patients, I instruct them to use alternative methods, i.e., distracting activities—such as talking with family and friends, engaging in a hobby, or using rational thinking and reminding themselves the benefits of alcohol abstinence and the consequence of alcohol use. In addition, if the urges of alcohol/drug use are strong and insistent, I use *Urge Surfing*. This technique allows the patient to focus on the urge to use it systematically until the surge passes. (Urge Surfing is associated with the ocean waves that start small, grow in size, and then break up and dispel.)

Communication and Problem Solving Skills— Through modeling, role-playing, and feedback, I teach my patients to use verbal and nonverbal skills (i.e., quality voice, appropriate language, facial expressions, etc.) in order to acquire good skills acquisition to solve problems. They identify the problem and then consider potential various solutions, selecting the most promising and appropriate approach and implementing it. Furthermore, my patients learn to function independently in a calm, collective, and easy manner and feel appreciated upon the solution of the problem.

Anger Awareness and Management—This is a very essential tool for the chemical substance abusing adolescents who are normally in conflict with many adults, such as parents, caretakers, educators, law, etc. The goal of anger management is to teach them to be aware and recognize their own angry thoughts and feelings and learn to convey them in a manner that is not harmful to them or others. Through role-playing, I teach my patients to demonstrate their internal negative reactions in an assertive manner versus an aggressive response. In this case, I ask them to use calming reminder phrases such as count out to ten, or verbalize the negative consequences of anger.

Negative Mood and Depression—There is a significant connection between substance abuse, depression, and other mood disorders. Some of the effective techniques that I employ to help my teen patients to control their debilitating emotions are:

- *Think more positively about the world and self.*

- *Become aware of self-defeating thoughts and respond to*

these thoughts with more realistic ones; act out these new thoughts.

In addition, I engage my patients' families in conjoint therapy, where they learn to better understand chemical substance use, recognize and identify their children's substance use symptoms and behaviors in order to intercept relapse, accept the importance of their supportive role in the process of treatment, and enhance their awareness and efforts in preventing *enabling* of relapse by taking over their children's responsibilities, or shielding them from the consequences of their behaviors. I also address the family's emotional burden and help the members to acquire coping skills that will lessen debilitating feelings (i.e., anger, fear, anxiety, and depression), which may interfere and endanger their children's treatment. I find conjoint family therapy to be an integral and influential factor in my patients' successful treatment. The family's emotional recovery resuscitates the relations of members, stabilizes the homeostasis of the family and allows the parents/caretakers to concentrate in their children's recovery through nurturing and accessibility of healthy and fun family opportunities.

Nothing would give me more satisfaction as an individual and professional to know that the information in this chapter convinced my readers how critical early therapeutic intervention is for all individuals and especially the youth that use/abuse alcohol and drugs without realizing their serious consequences. Children and teens that begin drinking and using other drugs before age fifteen are four times more at risk to become dependent on those chemical substances than those who do not use alcohol and drugs before age twenty-one. The failure to treat young chemical substance users early will contribute to incessant alcohol and drug use/abuse and eventually turn into addiction, a substance dependency disorder.

Circumstances can get worse if treatment is delayed and the young individuals suffer from substance induced psychiatric disorders (i.e., mood and psychotic disorders, anxiety disorders, sleep and eating disorders) caused by alcohol, marijuana, opiates, and other substances, they become resistant to treatment. This occurs because of their pathologic condition that distorts their awareness. Consequently, they are in denial, reject treatment or fail to follow through therapy. In this case, their substance abuse/dependency has to first be addressed and then their mental issues. In-patient rehabilitation treatment is recommended, incorporating strong psycho educational programs and self-help group participation. These programs teach resistance to chemical substance use/abuse through the emphasis of the physical, psychological, emotional, and social negative effects; strategies and techniques in maintaining sobriety; and introduction of patients to self-help groups (i.e., AA, NA). In many cases, anti-chemical substance craving medications may be used, but this may place the patients at high risk if they are on anti-psychotic medications. These patients require close monitoring and must be psychotically stabilized before they are introduced to chemical substance treatment.

The significant gain harvested from this chapter

is the realization that prevention of alcohol/drug use through education, positive modeling, and early treatment services are the most effective ways to interrupt teens' progression to later pathological alcohol and drug addiction, which frequently leads to the manifestation of substance-induced psychiatric disorders. The following are some of the signs and symptoms that may warn alcohol/drugs involvement.

Physical Signs: Fatigue; red and glazed eyes; unexplained weight loss; evidence of use (e.g., dilated/pinpoint pupils, tremors, perspiring, slurred/rapid speech, and tachycardia); inflamed, eroded nasal septum; lasting cough; and repeated health complaints

Emotional Signs: Low self-esteem; poor judgment; personality changes; feel that everyone is against them; general lack of interest(s); exhibit immediacy and impulsivity; more aggressive, violent, and assaultive behaviors; frequent depression and discouragement; attempted suicide or threats to hurt self; and self-mutilation

Family Signs: Argumentative; easily offended or defensive; resents authority; noncompliant to rules; secretiveness and things noticeably missing around the house; family communications become short and frank; stays away from home frequently; running away from home; and selling personal or family possessions

Social Signs: Friends become top priority or sudden change in friends; replace friends with new ones that make poor decisions and are not interested in family or school activities; changes to less conventional styles in dress and music; becomes involved in cult activities; and faces law problems

School Problems: Decreased interest in school; negative attitude toward school work and drop in grades; many truancy and absences; and discipline problems followed with multiple suspensions

Readers, please be aware that the above listed signs may be related to other problems. Although parents/caretakers tend to recognize signs of trouble in their children, it is advised that they consult their children's physician followed by a mental health professional (Focus Adolescents Services, 2006).

Chapter 5

Help Children to Stand Firm Against Alcohol and Other Drugs

Parents, you are the spark of life
That ignites my mind
I trust you will stand by
In the bewildered days of my life.

—Anthony Nicholas Betances,
Recognized National Poet

As I mentioned in my previous chapters, alcohol and drugs are a complex and serious problem, which affects not only the user but also all societal institutions that the user comes in contact with. Since this book is dedicated to preventing children's involvement in alcohol and drug use, this chapter will discuss an array of diverse means and approaches that the children's *micro systems* (immediate environment)—home, parent/caregiver, friends and teachers—can propagate to empower them against alcohol/drug use. In addition, it will look into the children's *macro systems* (cultural influences)—society in general, government, religious, and political systems—that are highly influential throughout the development of children and their transition to adolescence.

Home—Parents/Caregivers

Research shows that parents and caregivers are the strongest influence, especially at early ages, for preventing children from succumbing to the alcohol/drug culture. Unfortunately, a small percentage of children learn from their parents/caregivers about the harms of all forms of substance abuse. In order for parents or caregivers to be positive effecters to the children's anti-alcohol/drug attitudes and behaviors, they must have a wide knowledge in the area of alcohol/drug communication skills and the ability to detect the signs of alcohol/drug use. This skillfulness would prepare and empower them to take immediate action and address their children's problems as early as possible. Even limited use of alcohol/drugs may expose children to a variety of negative consequences. There is no way to predict in advance with certainty which children will or will not become chemical substance dependents, even considering personality traits, heredity, or community influence. However, there is a plethora of approaches that we can employ to prevent children from becoming victims of alcohol/drug use and abuse. Impelled by the findings of extensive research and professional experience, the author believes that *good character building* is one of the most effective tools in the prevention of alcohol/drug use.

Good Character Building

As farmers prepare the soil before the planting of the crops, similarly parents, caregivers, educators, and all those that are involved in children's lives have to prepare children's minds and hearts in order to be receptive and willing to actualize the teachings and the values pertaining to a healthy and dignified life free of alcohol and drugs. *Good character* has always been associated with alcohol/drug prevention and other negative and harmful behaviors that rob our young people's positive opportunities, which would make them healthy and productive individuals. Good character is the nature or make up of a person that makes him/her a responsible and compassionate individual, a person that contributes positively to the world. Good character embeds *ethic values, the knowledge of goodness, value of goodness*, and the *inner drive* to act upon it. A person with good character lives within the spectrum of *ethic values* and possesses high *self-esteem*, which reflects upon traits such as kindness, honesty, truthfulness, respect, responsibility, courage, leadership, citizenship, and other noble traits. Since self-esteem has been proven to be the core of good character, the following information is vivid proof of its dominant influence on children's behaviors throughout the course of their lives.

Self-Esteem—An individual's judgment of himself/ herself has a direct influence on how a person would live throughout life. Dorothy Briggs in her book, *Your Child's Self-Esteem*, states, "Self-esteem is the mainspring that states every child for success or failure as a human." Indeed, self-esteem is the wholesome sense of a person that would have a direct effect on how he/ she navigates life in the choices he/she would make in all aspects of life, friendships, marriage, relationships, occupation, stability, and if he/she would choose to become a leader or a follower. As we are aware, self-esteem is not developed through nature alone, but it is developed with the interactions of parents, family, and the world around the child. Furthermore, its development is consistently burdened with physical, emotional, and social challenges. However, there are life positive opportunities and experiences that endorse feelings of worth. The mastery of these developmental tasks generates and inspires high levels of self-esteem instantly as they are achieved.

Self-Esteem Fostering and Its Rewards—As I mentioned above, parents and caregivers are the architects that design the foundations where children build their self-esteem. That is children learn to view their thinking, feelings, and behaviors through those who are closely involved in the early years of their lives. Therefore, if children are regarded positively by their parents/caretakers, they will learn to envision their thoughts, emotions, and attitudes in a healthy manner and thus will be content and confident. Dr. Nathaniel Branden, a psychotherapist and publisher of numerous books on self-esteem, views self-esteem as the confidence in one's ability to think, learn, choose, and make appropriate decisions; the confidence to be happy and in the belief that achievement, success, friendships, respect, love, and fulfillment are appropriate to us. Parents and caregivers must understand and recognize the value of positive self-esteem in their children's lives in order to foster and reinforce its noble traits though genuine, caring, creative, and rewarding opportunities and experiences. Thus, when their children are faced with challenging situations, such as whether or not to use alcohol/drugs or to engage in other delinquent and destructive behaviors, they will be prepared to make the right and wise decisions for their own interest.

Children with very low self-esteem and peer approval of drug use at age eleven were found to have a high risk of drug dependency during their young adult years according to a study published by the University of Miami, Florida. In contrast, individuals with high self-esteem display lower levels of serious involvement with chemical substances as well as decreased tendency to experiment with them. If parents sense that their young teens suffer from low self-esteem and experimenting with chemical substances, they should engage them in prevention programs that through education and self-image therapy may produce changes in the teens' attitudes and behaviors toward chemical substance use. It is much easier to prevent youth from ever engaging in the use of chemical substances than it is to dissuade that use once it has begun. Adolescents that suffer from poor self-esteem and alcohol/drug dependency are hard to be treated because their personal efficacy, decision-making and communication skills are not adequately developed to make decisions for their own interest. This is very alarming for all parents and caretakers and necessitates their utmost efforts in fostering a healthy self-esteem in their children. The following recommendations and guidelines may be a useful resource for this significant undertaking.

Recommendations and Guidelines for Parents and Caretakers

Being parents or caregivers, you are wholly sited to influence and shape your children's views about themselves. Below are some practical strategies that you may use to foster self-esteem in your children that would deter them from chemical substance use and other harmful behaviors.

Model for your children a healthy (authentic) self-esteem. Let them know that you feel good about yourself; demonstrate to them that your self-worth is not entirely dependent on outside forces, for example, what other thinks about you (Green, S., 2006).

Convey your values. You should be the first person to talk with your children about drugs, violence, etc., before they become confused with somebody else's explanations that lack the sense of moral principles you would like to foster.

Show how much you care about your children; tell them that you love them. Spend quality time with them; listen with patience when they speak. By listening patiently, you allow children to express their own thoughts and feelings at their own pace, and furthermore you demonstrate to them that they are worthy of your time.

Reward your children for their good deeds with special privileges, or increase responsibility for a successful performance.

Take their emotions, ideals, and feelings seriously; do not disparage them. Avoid criticism that takes the form of ridicule or shame (i.e., calling children names, such as lazy, incompetent, stupid, etc.) or yelling, especially in front of their peers (Nuttal, P., 1991).

Define limits and rules clearly, and enforce them. If your rules are not clearly stated and understood, it allows a lot of room for misunderstanding, conflicts, and even manipulations. Establish logical consequences for inappropriate behaviors. Use consequences that have deterrent value and significant meaning to your children. The severity of the consequences should match the severity of the violation.

Teach your children to develop tolerance toward those that come from different cultural backgrounds or norm and to consider the feelings of others as important as their own.

Help children cope with negative feedback or frustrations by communicating to them that success on every occasion is not possible; share some personal experience from your own life (Katz, L., 1995).

Let us not overlook that there are other significant and effective tools that parents/caregivers and all those that are involved in children's lives may use to prevent alcohol and drug prevention. Positive outcome is often achieved through good *communication skills, responsibility, resiliency,* and *good decision-making.*

Communication Skills—Communication means to understand the other person's point of view, or the way he/she looks at the world, and even tactic desires and goals. When communication is harmonious and genuine, the words tend to reflect the feelings of the speaker. Effective communication involves both speaking and listening. A good listener should have the ability not only to receive the message of the other person, but also the ability to give feedback to the speaker, through verbal encouragement and facial expressions that show interest. Parents, caregivers, and educators that spend more time with children have been proven to be a powerful example of good communications.

Ideas for Improving Your Communication Skills

Demonstrate interest and attention to your children's conversations by the way you respond to them. For example, when children attempt to relate an alcohol/drug incident that they overheard in school, don't brush it off because you don't want to miss your favorite TV program. Take advantage of this teachable moment, and employ your alcohol/drug prevention skills by using an age appropriate dialogue.

Encourage children to talk—Children love an adult audience and enjoy sharing their ideas, thoughts, and feelings. They feel important and learn to become good conversationalists. Researchers support that children as well as adults that possess good communication skills are more likely to establish satisfying relationships. Thus, they would not feel lonely and isolated, both deeply painful emotions that often lead people into alcohol and drug use, and especially the youth that values friendships.

Listen to your children's nonverbal messages—Observe their facial expressions and body posture, tone of voice and changes in their demeanor. For example, when your children appear upset because their friends were accused for a wrongdoing action, take the time and inquire about the situation without being judgmental.

Avoid belittling your children—Do not humiliate them by pointing out their mistakes in a way to cause embarrassment or using sarcasm and ridicule. Labeling is injurious to *self-esteem*, which is one of the strongest antagonists of chemical substance use/abuse.

Reflecting feelings—Empathize with your children, and try to understand their thoughts and feelings. When children experience powerful emotional feelings that they are not fully aware of, it is practical and beneficial to rephrase or restate what they said. For example, you may reflect children's feelings by saying, "It must hurt you being yelled at by your coach in the game." If the parents demonstrate empathy, their children are more likely to learn to be empathic too. That may restrain them from future destructive behaviors, such as chemical substance use, theft, violence, etc., taking into consideration the hurt that it may cause to their parents and all those that care for them.

Communicate your values and expectations clearly— Parents are the closest persons to their children and should be the first ones to discuss with them difficult subjects, such as alcohol/drugs, violence, or other touching issues. Do not allow your children to learn about some serious topics from other people that do not carry your values and principles. Research supports that children need moral guidance from their parents and do not hesitate to state your beliefs in a clear manner. Remember "drinking and drugs" are critical topics and should not be a one-time conversation. Start at an early age with clear and age-appropriate explanations in order to avoid confusion and the risk to provide more complicated information that your young children's minds cannot comprehend. Thus, when your children reach their teen years, they will already have the basic knowledge to understand and internalized higher levels of information and facts associated with the paramount risk and consequences of alcohol/drug use. For example, teens have to know which drugs pose the most risks, that mixing certain substances can be deadly, and that driving under the influence or attending school under the influence should never be an option in their lives. In addition, parents need to convey and convince their teens that they are whole-heartedly committed to their welfare.

Responsibility

This powerful trait develops a sense of personal power permitting children to feel capable and confident. It helps them to be aware of themselves and their own actions contributing to what happens in their lives and what they do makes a difference. In order to teach the sense of responsibility, you must model and provide appropriate opportunities through which your children will conceptualize, understand, and internalize this essential trait. The development of responsibility is an ongoing process that requires diverse skills to meet the needs of the children, whose responsibilities increase and become more complex as they grow. Infusing children and young adults with a sense of personal responsibility and showing them the result of good and bad choices should be every parent's goal of parental achievement (Child and Development Institute, 2006). Some of the examples below may enlighten the parents/caretakers to better understand why responsibility is so important for children (starting at a young age), what essential and effective skills and approaches can be utilized that will empower them to become responsible individuals with a repelling disposition toward alcohol and drugs.

Instilling Responsibility

Considering children's ages, assign them tasks/chores that they can successfully achieve. For example, young children should take care of their hygiene needs, do their homework and chores, and go to bed at the designated time; teens should adhere to their school's policies and regulations, assist in house chores, and not break their curfew rules. Children should always be supported and encouraged for their responsible actions and deeds and be praised for their willingness to help. Reward your children's accomplishments, but do not bribe them in order to persuade them do something that you expect them to do.

Teach children to make good decisions, which are essential life skills for survival, success, and happiness. Give children a reference plan, which will help them to take the necessary steps in order to make their decision(s).

Steps—Identify the problem or situation; think about all the possible approaches you could employ to solve the problem; take into consideration the possible consequences (positive or negative) to each action; make your decision; and consider the outcome; be prepared to attempt another possible solution.

Teach and prepare children to take responsibility for their actions in decision-making by accepting all consequences. For example, being honest by accepting responsibility if they made a bad decision, if they lie or camouflage their actions, and apologize if the decision hurts another person.

Teach and model children to control and handle their impulses by reminding them the possible outcomes and consequences and acknowledge their feelings (i.e., say, "I see you have been hurt, upset, or sad"). Impulsivity is a temperamental risk factor for substance use. As we know, impulsive children often suffer from poor self-esteem, immaturity, critical thinking, and poor judgment. Therefore, they are vulnerable to surrender to alcohol and drugs, which follow them from a very young age.

Teach and model children to handle conflicts peacefully by using the previously described decision-making approach and role-playing. Remind them that unsolved conflicts often lead to all sorts of violence and generally hurt all parties involved.

Teach children to resist peer pressure by reminding them of the negative events that may happen to them if they cave in to their friends' negative whims. Children spend an increasing amount of time in peer interactions during middle and late childhood and adolescence. In typical school days, there are approximately 275 episodes with peers. Responsible children tend to be less enticed to their peers' alcohol/drug pressure and other destructive anti-social behaviors (Pilon, R., 2004). Since peer pressure is so critical when it comes to children's alcohol/drug involvement, it will be wise to convey to your children that good friends share their feelings and values and respect each other's good decisions. Thus, you will help your children to understand that friends that press them to drink and use drugs are not worthy of their friendship. That will increase the chance of staying away from them and not be involved in their alcohol and drug escapades.

Set specific, clear, and firm rules, but make sure that they are fair. If the parents' rules are not clearly stated and understood that may lead to misunderstanding, conflicts, and even manipulations. Rules also should be consistently enforced. Children and especially teens need to know they can depend on their parents and caretakers. If the rules are broken, the established consequences should be enforced immediately. Researchers show that teens are less prone to use alcohol and drugs if their parents set clear rules dictating to stay away from chemical substance. In addition, teens with unsupervised time are three times more likely to use marijuana, drink under age, and be sexually active than other teens.

Of course, there are other critical factors that place children and teens on the front line of the alcohol and drug war. For example, the inability of understanding, recognizing, expressing, and controlling emotions has been acknowledged to be an indisputable influence on the adolescents' poor decisions related to alcohol and drug use. Parents, teachers, and all those that are in the children's lives, be indebted to teach them to identify and process their feelings in order to be responsible for their choices. Starting with young children, teach them to verbalize and identify their feelings, and as they become older to gain ownership of them. Through age appropriate dialogues, role-playing, skits, stories, and life's experience make children and teens realize that emotions are part of themselves and they are responsible for the way they express and control them.

Expressing Emotions

It is a life's necessity for our children and teens, as well as for adults, to know how to process and properly handle feelings in order to build resiliency against alcohol and drug use and many other deleterious incitements. Home and school are the most appropriate places where emotions may be learned, fostered, and properly handled. Children that have acquired the knowledge and expression of feelings, through their parents' modeling and teaching and school's reinforcement, have better skills to constructively practice them in making decisions that will be advantageous to their future. Unfortunately, there are many children and teens today that lack the skills and opportunities of processing and expressing their emotions, either because their feelings have been anesthetized due to physical, emotional, and psychological abuse and neglect or as a result of absence of appropriate teaching and processing. Inclusive research shows that children and teens that come from these harsh and uncaring environments generally are powerless and defenseless when they are exposed to the lure of alcohol/drugs as well as to the pressures of other adverse situations and circumstances.

It is the obligation and responsibility of parents/caregivers, educators, and all others involved in the lives of the children to teach them to effectively regulate and appropriately use their emotions in all life situations and settings. That will decrease their susceptibility to chemical substance use as well as other harmful engagements. The forthcoming writing conveys effective strategies and techniques that will help our children and especially teens to control powerful negative feelings that may lead them to serious trouble.

Stress and How to Help Children to Cope with It

Stress is our body's response to any stimulus. Any type of stress triggers physiological responses that cause our adrenaline output to increase, our heart to pump faster and our breathing rate to elevate. However, if these body responses are not properly channeled over a period of time, they may become negative stress and harm our being.

The Oxford English Dictionary defines negative stress as hardship, adversity and affliction. In simple words, stress is a short form for distress that is an essential part of our lives and responsible for many physical and psycho-emotional related diseases. In the United States, by some estimates, the economic burden of stress related to illness exceeds 200 billion annually (McEwen & Lasley, 2002, chapter 1). When we become stressed out, all the body systems, brain, glands, hormones, immune system, heart, blood, lungs, and liver work synergistically in order to defend our organism. This stress response, known as the *fight-or-flight response*, helps us to react to an emergency and cope with change. But when our body is overwhelmed or disrupted, then the stress response system begins to engender physical and emotional conditions that accelerate illnesses. Examples of physical illnesses may be heart attacks and strokes, allergies, ulcers, gastrointestinal problems, fatigue syndrome, etc. The brain is as well victimized when the feelings of stress are unpredictable, overpowering and last for a long time. Severe stress sensitizes neural pathways and makes parts of the brain that are involved in responses to stress and fears (i.e., limbic system, hippocampus, and amygdala) to overwork. When these areas of the brain are stimulated frequently and for long periods, other brain regions that are involved in complex thought and immune system response are put off. Then, the body sights stressful events as "fight-or-flight" crisis situations, where protecting oneself from the stressor(s) takes priority over other brain responses and bodily processes (Sapolsky, 1993).

Stress, in our demanding society, exerts infinite pressures on the lives of children, whose defense system is crumbling due to the overloading social activities and commitments, competitively academic performance, peer influence, alcohol/drug subculture invasion, and other social stressors that cause malfunction of the *fight-or-flight response.*

Overloading Social Activities and Commitments—As an educator for twenty years, I have observed a large number of children involved in more then three sports or other organized activities at the same time, while they struggle to keep up with their school's demands. A large number of these children suffer from sleep deprivation, are irritable, moody, and often fall asleep during class. Research in the University of Chicago found that lack of sleep interferes with health responses to stressors and impedes the immunity system. On the contrary, a good night's sleep (ten hours) relaxes the neuron-system, promotes restorative processes throughout the body, and improves memory and concentration. Conversely, as a mental health therapist, I have treated a respectful number of adolescents and college athletes for anxiety disorders related to pressure and physical/emotional stress caused by overpowering and conceited coaches, who forget that athletes are also individuals with different abilities and learning paths. Honestly, we need more entrusted coaches with good communication skills, flexibility, understanding, and commitment to the students' welfare.

Parents and caretakers need to prioritize their children's needs by accepting their human limitations and not overloading them with extracurricular activities (athletic sports, dance, acting, etc.) that deprive them of family interaction, free creative playing, resting, and sleeping. Coaches and all others that are involved in the physical, intellectual, or social development of children and teens, through sports, leadership, or other extra curriculum disciplines, need to encourage and support students' efforts though generous praise, honesty, fairness, and avoiding criticism. Thus, they will give them the opportunity to reach their potential by improving their skills, enhancing their talents, and building self-esteem. Consequently, they will be able to mitigate stressful situations and conditions that trigger unhealthy moods (i.e., irritability, anxiety, anger, depression, etc.), which frequently drive individuals and especially young people to deceiving escapes, such as alcohol and drugs and other debilitating behaviors.

Moods—They are mental dispositions that affect the way an individual thinks and feels about something and how he/she reacts. For example, if a person is verbally attacked by someone, he/she may feel humiliated, become hurt and withdrawn, or angry and physically aggressive. This indicates that moods are like a swinging pendulum, and they may go from high to low, depending on how they are processed. Children as well as adults, whose self-image has eroded and are trapped in unmanageable mood swings, are doomed to make inappropriate decisions that consequently lead to destructive behaviors.

Helping children to develop positive mood maintenance skills is critical and should start at an early age. Children, who have formed a "secured attachment" with their primary caregivers, through safe, comfort and trusting relationships, are predicted to have a better psychological well being, such as a higher self-esteem and lower levels of mood swing (Cooper & et. al., 1998). As adolescents, they tend to be more empathetic, forgiving, and have better communication and problem-solving decision skills. In contrast, children with *insecure attachment* as a result of an unpredictable and unstable caregiver environment, as they grow up have poor regulated moods, which facilitate intolerance, anger, resentment, and conflictual interactions. Teens as well as adults that have not acquired healthy mood processing skills find themselves to be emotionally and psychologically unstable, have difficulty coping with the demands of life and often tend to self-medicate their moods through the use of alcohol and drugs. In addition, they are at high risk to develop mood disorders if their erratic moods are not addressed at an early age.

It is a proven fact that healthy child rearing is closely linked to emotional stability, a strong barrier to alcohol/drug use and abuse. Keeping this undisputable message in mind, use your nurturing tools to foster and regulate your children's emotions that would prepare them to face the adversities and threats of life and not surrender to alcohol and drugs. I have stressed the importance of healthy emotion-processing and good decision-making in the prevention of alcohol/drugs. However, there are other essential variables that may rejuvenate children's and adolescents' cognition, stabilize their emotions and illuminate their mental process in making good decisions when they are exposed to alcohol and drugs. Some factors that may affect our children's and especially our adolescents' decision-making choices in life may be: *good nutrition, exercises, meditation and relaxation, sufficient sleep,* and *relaxation techniques.* The practice of these necessities may break the vicious cycle of stress, mood swings, and depression, all of which have been proven to predispose individuals to alcohol and drug use.

Good Nutrition

What we eat may affect the way we feel. The various nutrients in the food that we ingest may affect our body's chemistry, which in return may cause changes in our moods. However, there are ways that we can control harmful moods, for example, stress, anxiety, withdrawal, emptiness, etc., through the use of appropriate and healthy foods. We can reduce our stress by eating whole grain products, beans, and vegetables that boost the production of serotonin, a mood stabilizer. Whole-grain foods, milk, organ meats, fortified cereals and breads that enhance energy production in the brain cells may improve irritability and anxiety. Depression may be prevented by eating chicken, beef, potatoes, oats, broccoli, tomato products, and egg yolk (Maurizio, 2006). Dr. Mischoulon, director of Alternative Remedy Studies at the Depression Clinical and Research Program at Massachusetts General Hospital, recommends that adults as well as children should receive the nutrients they need from eating a balanced diet. Since most of our children do not eat a balanced diet, it would be a sensible idea to place them on vitamins. Supplements should be recommended by a medical professional and intelligently used.

Parents and caretakers can teach their children to learn healthy eating habits that they will follow for the rest of their lives. Below are some helpful tips that will encourage and teach your children to appreciate healthy foods.

Sharing meals as a family can actually improve children's food habits and give them the opportunity to learn more about the benefits of healthy foods. Children tend to eat more fruits, vegetables, and dairy food at meals shared with their parents.

Do not give up easily when you introduce a healthy new food to your children and they refuse to accept it. Involve them in the planning and preparing the meals. Children tend to eat the foods that they prepare. Encourage them to watch advertisements that promote healthy foods and not high fat snacks, sugar drinks, and sugary cereals.

Make sure that your children have breakfast daily. Breakfast is one of the most important meals of the day because it provides children with the energy they need to start the day and cope with the demands of school.

Limit the amount of added sugar; avoid added sweeteners in your children's diet. Although there is contradictory research as to the correlation between sugar and children's hyperactive behavior, personally being with children for twenty years, I have found even passive children to be over-stimulated, irritable, and cranky when their diets include concentrated sources of sugar, like fruit juice, soda, jam, syrup, etc. These types of refined carbohydrates tend to create radical spikes in the blood sugar level, which make them feel moody. Nutritionists recommend the use of foods rich in soluble fiber, which have the ability to absorb sugar in the blood and potentially lessen blood sugar and mood swings. They also recommend foods rich in omega-3 fats, like fish (salmon and sardines), canola oil, walnuts, and omega-3 fortified flaxseed, borage, and safflower oil, all of which have been thoroughly researched and found to alleviate depression (Bauer, 2006).

Exercises

The American Holistic Association, an organization of physicians devoted to the medical care of the whole person, as well as a respectful number of medical doctors, suggests that exercises are the natural enhancers in the stabilizing of human moods. Studies indicated that both aerobic exercise and vigorous training considerably reduce depressive symptoms. Researchers of Duke University Medical Center, divided 156 depressed subjects into three treatment groups, A, B, & C. *A* group used a treadmill or stationary bicycle for thirty minutes, three times a week; *B* group used antidepressant treatment with Zoloft; and *C* group used a combined treatment of antidepressants and exercise. Originally, the group that took only Zoloft (B group) improved faster, but within sixteen weeks of treatment, all three groups received the same benefits. That means that exercise was proven to be as therapeutic as antidepressant therapy.

I have noticed that an increasing number of children do not engage in physical activity on a regular basis. Inactivity is more prevalent among girls than boys, and the level of physical activity declines as children become older. According to the Center of Diseases and Control, Youth Risk Behavior Surveillance during the year 2005, 45 percent of the ninth grade students and only 22 percent of the twelfth grade students attended physical education class on a daily basis. I would recommend an exercise family program, which fits your daily schedule and your children's, be adopted and be part of your daily routine. Instead of allowing your children to watch TV and play video games, engage them in fun activities. Be a model, be active together with your children, take a walk, ride a bike, play ball, play catch, or gardening. Not only your children will increase their energy and enhance their healthy mood, but they will also have the opportunity to spend some quality time and will be emotionally better connected with you.

Scientists have discovered that physical activity can affect a number of mood altering brain chemicals (i.e. dopamine, norepinephrine, and serotonin). Many of my patients have reported that when they exercise they manage to better control their anxiety, are calmer, and solve conflicts in a more amicable manner. The Journal of American Medical Association reports that light to moderate exercises, three ten-minute periods (daily) can be as beneficial as one thirty-minute session. Exercises increase self-esteem and prevent anxiety and stress across all ages and particularly in adolescents who are risk takers and often expose themselves to alcohol and drug experimentation.

Overview of Meditation and Relaxation

Meditation and relaxation strategies have shown to reduce anxiety and stress. They also reduce feelings of anger, confusion, tension, and fatigue, all of which may trigger chemical substance abuse. Both facilitate sleep and help to fall asleep if you wake during the night. Dr. Herbert Benson, a pioneer in the medical application of practical meditation, found that meditation lowers the body's metabolism, reduces blood lactic acid (the stress-related blood chemical), and highly reduces the nervous system tension.

Meditation—The preparedness of the mind is one of the prerequisites of meditation. In other words, the mind should be eager to rest for meditation and should not feel any kind of force. Most people feel a difficulty in getting any type of satisfactory results from meditation, because their minds are not prepared. The need for the practice of meditation should be a genuine one. Consequently the soul-filled with absorption of affection and love would generate the inner harmony that would bring peace. The following is an example of a simple meditation technique that you may train your teens to use daily.

Choose an environment free from distractions and activities. Have your teens sit on a chair in a comfortable position with their feet touching the ground. Instruct your teens to close their eyes and request something that they want from their super power (i.e., implore for help to handle a school problem or a friendship issue); pose for a few seconds, and then relax by listening to their breathing. As your teens concentrate on the breathing, ask them to choose a personal affirmation (i.e., I believe in myself, I am confident, I am responsible, I am determined, and I will get out of trouble or solve the conflict with my friend in a positive manner), slowly repeating it to themselves at least eight times and calmly listening to their repetition. Gradually, your teens will start to sense less tension and anxiety and a realm of peaceful thoughts and feelings will flow into their minds. Upon completion of the affirmations, ask your teens to continue breathing calmly until serenity engulfs their entire being. Your teens may open their eyes (while they take a calm breath) and enjoy their tranquility.

Relaxation—Relaxation can produce wonderful benefits for young children whose feelings are naïve and cannot identify their moods. For younger children parents/caretakers you may use relaxation activities, such as coloring; drawing; watercolor painting; and building models with Legos and blocks; assembling airplanes, boats, and car models; playing Tick Tack Toe, Scrabble, and Connecting Four; flying rockets and kites; racing cars and tracks; blowing bubbles and balloons; reading humorous stories; listening to the music; looking at family pictures and videos; and other fun activities. All the above proposed relaxation techniques have shown to calm down and control high-range moods of irritability, anxiety, and anger. Thus, the children learn from very young age to identify their negative moods, realize that they can be controlled in many positive, fun, and productive ways before they become internalized and take over their personality and life. In general, young moody children when they reach adolescence and adulthood are at high risk to experiment and use alcohol and drugs.

Of course, there are other effective and beneficial relaxation techniques that are used by many mental health professionals for adolescents as well as for adults. Some of them are: *controlled breathing, visual or pleas-*

ant imagery, and *mindfulness.* I frequently practice these mind and body relaxation techniques with my adolescent patients as well as adult patients. I have also trained my patients to employ them when they feel threatening by their moods, such as stress, tension, anxiety, anger, sadness, sleeping disturbances, all of which increase the risk of chemical substance use/abuse. The following constitutes some paradigms of the above-mentioned techniques that you can learn to use with your children when you detect them to be overwhelmed with school demands, peer and social pressures, and other life challenges, which are known as beguiling invitations to alcohol and drug use.

Control Breathing—This is a simple technique and can be beneficial in many diverse situations. Controlled breathing helps to relax and reduce tension by slowing down breathing. Before you engage your children in this technique, instruct them to be aware of their breathing (each breath in and out counts as one) and concentrate on a calming word (i.e., relax, rose, lamb, blue, etc). Then, have them slowly inhale for four seconds through the nose and slowly exhale for four seconds through the mouth (let breath flow smoothly), while thinking the calming word and imagining the tension flowing out of the entire body. Ask your children to repeat this exercise for at least six times. It might take a few practices until they recognize the benefits of the breathing technique and learn to use it on their own when the need arises (Sharp, J., 2006).

Visual or Pleasant Imagery—This approach revokes feelings of calmness and serenity and helps the partici-

pant to deal with all sorts of stressful situations. Before
you use this technique, have your teens relax in a comfortable chair, in a quiet environment. Then, proceed by
asking your teens (with their eyes closed) to use their
imagination (the mind's eyes) and envision themselves
in a serene and beautiful location, i.e., a calm beach or
a lake, a colorful garden, or on top of a high plateau.
In a low and calm tone of voice, guide them to feel
the gentle waves of the ocean caressing their feet, smell
the aroma of the lilies through the swirling air, and
see the dazzling sun as it glistens on top of the snowy
white mountain. Encourage your teens to calm down
and allow these tranquil images to become permanent
mental pictures in their visual memories and return to
them whenever they sense high nervous energy stress
to invade their being. I personally use this technique,
and I have found it to be less stressful and more ener-
getic to combat the daily hassles of life.

Mindfulness—It means to be in control of your mind.
Learn how to reflect on a thought or emotion before
taking action. Mindfulness facilitates mental health,
stress reduction, anger management, and self-discovery.
It helps one to understand and know how to respond to
life challenges with a calm and clear mind. Mindfulness
teaches self-awareness and can be a conscientious navigator in the adolescents' lives, which are challenged by
negative behaviors, such as violence, crime, alcohol, and
drugs. It is a powerful tool of self-introspection through
which the teens may discover their inner strengths and
abilities and use them to make the right choices in

decision-making for present and future life situations, and especially for alcohol and drug resistance.

Dr. Marshal Linehan, an American psychologist, who has developed and written helpful materials on the subject of mindfulness, states that in order for individuals and especially children to achieve mindfulness, they need to be taught the following skills: observe, describe, and participate in a presenting experience.

• Observe—Being attentive to experience and not hasty; be just in touch with their thoughts and sensations (i.e., feeling their body on the soft mattress).

• Describe—Be able to verbalize and label what is observed by only providing truthful information (i.e., I see the baby walking, I see the car moving).

• Participate—Be totally engaged and emerged into an action (i.e., focusing their full awareness on chewing food well, noticing its taste and texture).

In addition, the successful employment of the above skills requires that mindful participants be:

• Non-judgmental—Not to allow their personal opinion to interfere with thoughts that will block constant acceptance and acknowledge of mindfulness.

• Focus—Concentrate on one thing at a time so that their action is not diverted (for example, when they are listening to music, they listen, and when they are drawing, they draw). Focus on being effective, think on what you are doing.

If you practice with your teens the above mindfulness skills, they will be part of their mental repertoire. Thus, they can be used as coping mechanisms against their daily pressures and stressful events of life, which challenge their youthful persona and often lead them to the road of substance abuse and other unhealthy behaviors.

How Schools Can Help Children
Resist Alcohol and Drugs

Although schools are strong advocates of alcohol and drug prevention and have developed and implemented a diverse variety of educational programs, their effects appear to be limited on a vast number of students who are experimenting/using all sorts of chemical agents.

After serving as substance awareness coordinator in various schools, I recognize that the implementation of empowering anti-drug/alcohol programs predispose strong commitment to their delivery. That means schools with encouraging and strong policies that reinforce and support an alcohol-free lifestyle for all students. Well-educated and motivated school staff should be not only familiar with the school's alcohol/drug prevention curriculum but also well trained to understand the personality and needs of their students, which are among the influential factors of chemical substances use. For example, students with early and persistent antisocial, aggressive, and irritable temperamental personality, sensation seeking and low sense of self-esteem are more likely to engage in alcohol and drug use. This high-risk population, parallel to regular academic curricula, should be taught good interpersonal skills and social competence by motivated and empathic teachers who possess positive managerial behavioral skills. Enthusiastic teachers who are self-driven and are controllers of their performance tend to inspire student's learning, while empathic and caring teachers have a better class control, which reduces student's stress and anger, both denoting triggers of chemical substance involvement.

It is a fact that there are a number of students who, although they do not exhibit any high risk of biologically predisposed or personality factors, still become victims of alcohol and drug use. Researchers support that (besides peer pressure, which already was discussed) academic pressure and extracurricular overload, generating high levels of unmanageable stress and anxiety, often drive adolescent students to chemical substance use for stress reduction.

Academic Pressure—Many high school students, parallel to taking college prep courses and striving for high grades, in order to put together an impressive portfolio for colleges, take many extra-curricular activities. As a result, they are overloaded with homework assignments, book reports, and studying for tests. These ambitious students are worrying to meet their goals and before realizing it become stressed out, anxious, and physically and mentally exhausted. Failing to meet their expected educational achievements, some of them may start using/abusing prescription drugs to boost their physical endurance and enhance their mental alertness, while others engage in drinking to cope with feelings of failure and defeat.

It is wise that every school be staffed with an apt number of well-trained academic counselors who are readily accessible to evaluate students' capabilities and potential before they allow these ambitious adolescents to overload their school schedules with extra curricular activities, such as theater rehearsals, dance classes, team sports, teen clubs, and teen board meetings. Students, who are active in so many pursuits, barely have time for their daily meals and for an adequate night's sleep, both necessary nutrients of body and mind and reducers of stress. School-based mental health and chemical substance prevention and intervention programs should be established in all schools where knowledgeable, competent, and empathic counselors teach the overworked students to control and manage their stress and anxiety by managing time wisely, planning in advance, and not rarely reconsidering the elimination of some extra curricular activities.

Schools being the vehicle of knowledge and societal trends should be the leading proponents in the anti-alcohol/drug prevention by encouraging, motivating and educating students to resist any chemical substance experimentation/use regardless of their educational capabilities, inspirations, peer pressure, and even psycho-emotional stamina. Anti-drug alcohol/drug educational programs, built into the school's general, daily curriculum, starting with early education, with a strong component of prevention skills and strategies, should be the schools' number one priority.

Universities and colleges should educate all potential teachers in the area of alcohol *and* drugs, with emphasis in the identification of early alcohol/drug use. Schools should institute in their policies *teacher mandatory reporting* of any suspicious alcohol/drug use involvement and immediately report it to the administration. Testing should be followed up. Teachers should be relinquished of any legal implications or consequences. If the schools adhere to such policies, I strongly believe that the student alcohol/substance use will be reduced and the schools' resistance against alcohol/drugs will be embraced by most of the school population.

Peer-to-peer intervention programs should be established and adopted by all schools starting from second grade. Such interventions have proved to be beneficial among young people who are more aware of each other's wants and needs due to age compatibility. Therefore, the risky youth might find understanding, compassion, and strength from these level-headed peers and not succumb to the internal and external temptations of their environment. Thus, they will escape the epidemic of chemical substance use/abuse, and they will follow the path of a healthy and promising life.

In addition, schools should offer mandatory family anti-alcohol/drug education for parents/caretakers, grandparents. Notice that large portions of children, especially among the economically deprived, are raised by grandparents today. Positive incentives should be given to the families that attend these programs, conducted after working hours. Examples of such incentives may be:

- *Credits to their children in school*

- *Preference in employment*

- *Public recognition*

- *Vouchers for alcohol/drug educational materials*

- *Free passes to healthy family fun activities.*

Society's Position in the Prevention of Alcohol and Other Drugs

Societies should also be accountable for the young people's alcohol/drug epidemic. Their political leaders and judicial and human systems should fully recognize the magnitude of the adolescence's chemical substance use/abuse and, therefore, take drastic actions to eradicate the problem. Unfortunately, our present society appears to be in denial and has failed to protect the youth from this widely spread epidemic. Some of the reasons contributing to this existing position are:
The laws that govern chemical substance traffic are not punitive enough to prevent the drugs before they reach our youth.

- Our judicial system is not harsh enough with those cases that involve soliciting drugs to adolescents.

• Competent, responsible, and committed individuals do not administer our juvenile alcohol and drug detention centers. Furthermore, they barely have moderate and effective educational and therapeutic programs.

• TV advertisements and family programs, newspapers and youth periodicals should be more thoroughly censored by the government for "hidden suggestive" alcohol and other drug promotions.

• The approval of new medications potentially of high addiction should be thoroughly tested by the FDA before they are approved and marketed.

• In order to improve and increase the availability of more effectively preventive chemical substance abuse programs for our youth, the government should increase their funding for the research of more reliable assessment tools for adolescent chemical substance abuse and other comorbid disorders, and effective maintenance sobriety programs. Such programs may be wellness-oriented programs that provide physical, mental, social, and spiritual activities and opportunities. Social activities centering on healthy, fun programs have been proved to be a dynamic tool for chemical substance prevention and treatment. These social programs should be free and available to youth and their families not only in the cities, but also in all remote rural areas.

The position of the government in the protection of our youth from the rapid spread of the social disease of chemical substance abuse should take a fast stand and leading role, overcoming political rivalries, and monitoring excuses. Our politicians in all levels, national and state, should encourage and financially support *advocacy* anti-alcohol/drug groups to attract more anti-alcohol/drug young people to join their efforts in reaching out to the high-risk young populations of chemical substance use. Examples of such vulnerable populations may be: *adolescents of high-risk families, dropout school students, adolescents in chemical substance recovery, DUI adolescents* (driving under the influence), and *adolescents with dual diagnosis* (i.e., chemical substance abuse and mood disorders).

Spiritual Institutions

We are living in an era of spiritual awakening and there is great hope for the tender minds of children to be candled by the sincere and committed teaching of spiritual and moralistic leaders. Those leaders must be models of alcohol and drug-free life in order for the adolescents to emulate and follow them in the combat of alcohol/drug temptations. Parents or caretakers should be the ones to encourage and lead their children from a very young age to legitimate spiritual institutions and practices, which are strong advocates of anti-alcohol/drug use and curtailers of other anti-social behaviors. Parallel, such institutions should be state-funded to hire qualified alcohol/drug professionals to provide free counseling and therapy to high-risk adolescents and their families that are susceptible to chemical substance use.

I hope the information and concepts of this chapter persuade readers that alcohol and drug prevention is one of the most crucial and significant missions that families, schools, and society as a whole must undertake in order to shield children from the bullets of the alcohol/drug war and secure for them an environment conducive to a healthy and productive life.

Conclusion

Look beyond every child's eyes
Get in touch with his feelings
And special dreams
And you will discover a passion for life so
You will never betray him.

—Author

I feel honored for having the opportunity to write *How to Shield Children from Alcohol and Other Drugs* because of its highly valuable content associated with the welfare of the most divine humans, our children. I strongly believe that its authenticity based on scientific studies, research, and empirical data will convince every reader that alcohol and drug prevention is the most effective way to eradicate our youth's deceiving perception that the use of these harmful drugs is a style of life.

If we understand the fragility of the tender minds and bodies of our young children, it is easy to acknowledge that *child rearing* is a critical factor for their normal development and behavior across the spectrum of life. Children nurtured by faithful, protective, dedicated, and positive model parents are more likely to enjoy not only a healthy childhood but a stable adolescence and a productive adulthood as well.

In contrast, those children who are reared in non-nurturing, unhealthy environments are at high risk to experience psycho-emotional problems and later on in life become victims of alcohol and drugs and other harmful behaviors. Young children's minds absorb any messages that come from those that they love and trust, for example, parents/caretakers and teachers. These messages are registered in their mental repertoire and transmitted into behaviors and attitudes. When children reach adolescence, the most challenging stage of physical, psycho-emotional, cognitive, and social development, and their mental schema are healthy will have a better chance to defend themselves from the temptations of alcohol and drugs. Adolescents whose rearing has been shadowed by mistrust, betrayal, deprivation of love, insecurity, and other painful experiences have a confused personality and often suffer from psycho-emotional problems, recognized triggers of chemical substance involvement. Not to mention the genetically predisposed children with first-degree relatives of alcoholism that run the risk three to four times higher to become addicts. Given the above facts, we cannot ignore that family rearing in the transition of childhood to adolescence is a challenging commitment for all those that are involved in children's lives.

Since the concepts of this book aim to awaken the conscience of parents, caretakers, teachers and all those that are involved in the welfare of children, I find it necessary to acquaint the readers with the most prevalent drugs, including alcohol, which are highly attractive to our children and especially to adolescence. When I speak about drugs, I refer to any chemical substance taken into the body by mouth, inhaled, injected, or rubbed on the skin that causes changes in the body and/or mind of the user.

Alcohol

I have extensively elaborated on the drug *alcohol*, which has been a serious concern to all professionals and researchers responsibly committed to the welfare of children. According to the National Council on Alcohol and Drugs, alcohol is one of the biggest drug problems in the U.S. and the number one killer among adolescents than all other fatal illnesses combined. The effects of alcohol are poly-dimensional and have serious negative impacts on the body and mind of the user as well as his/her family, school, and society where he/she lives. Alcohol depresses the body's immune system and makes the user vulnerable to all sorts of illnesses, including cancer, gastrointestinal problems, heart attacks, etc. Even small amounts of alcohol affect the brain, especially the adolescent's, which is extremely sensitive because it continues to develop through childhood and adolescence up to about age twenty. It produces a number of immediate effects such as: *Slows brain responses, impairs thought processes in the cerebral cortex, increases the likelihood of risky sexual behaviors, causes loss of memory, and heightens emotions, such as aggressiveness, sadness, and withdrawal.* It also *causes loss of fine motor control and balance,* and it *impairs the ability to transfer information into long-term memory storage.* Severe and prolonged alcohol users often develop *Wernick-Korsakoff Syndrome,* an irreversible brain damage, which leads to inability to remember new information for more than a few seconds. Alcohol also causes distortion of judgment, which is highly responsible for drunk driving. The Journal of the American Medical Association reported in 1993 that fatal vehicle accidents at night are three times more likely to occur by teens ages fifteen to twenty being under the influence of alcohol and drugs.

Adolescents' families experience the pain of their sons/daughters' alcohol/drugs escapades, which often lead in unsolved conflicts and even family disintegration. The Monitoring the Future, National Results on Adolescent Drug Abuse report of 2003 indicated that nearly 77 percent of students by the end of their high school years have consumed alcohol. A large number of them exhibited grade dropping, deteriorating behavior, and altering of future goals. Early alcohol/drug use has a heavy burden on society imposed by astronomic expenses associated with alcohol/drug treatment, sexually transmitted disease treatment, lawful expenses, educational prevention, alcohol/drug induced mental and physical illness, and so many other unnecessary expenditures generated from adolescents' alcohol/drug use and irresponsible behaviors.

Marijuana

Marijuana has been the most undermined drug in our society today. A large number of the general population and even some professionals disregard its use, by considering it less harmful than any other drug. As a result, this insidious drug has dominated our youth's life and is highly used by the school population, especially among students grades eight to ten. Marijuana's delta-9 tetrahydrocannobinol (THC) poisonous compound prevents the formation of DNA, proteins and other essential building blocks necessary for the growth of cells and their division. The THC in marijuana attacks the immune system and damages the cells and tissues in the body, opening its susceptibility to infections. Marijuana causes respiratory problems, including lung infections and pneumonia. It affects the brain, liver, and reproductive organs. Marijuana alters the secretion of hormones, which effect the metabolic changes and stress, causing anxiety, depression, and panic in the user. The Science Behavioral Pharmacology reports that marijuana affects *safe driving*. Data of *drunk driver* tests show that the lack of coordination among marijuana smoking drivers is equal to those drivers that have too much to drink.

Nicotine

Nicotine is the most toxic chemical of the tobacco plant. It is highly addictive, and its effects are dispelled within minutes of ingestion. This prompts the user to frequent smoking in order to maintain the drug's effect. Tobacco smoking is responsible for the death of at least 430,000 people in the U.S. each year. Its effects are associated with hazardous health problems, including premature death. Chronic smokers may develop *cancer* in major organs and body parts, for example, *lungs, stomach, kidney, bladder, skin,* and *cervix*. Nicotine in smoking releases dopamine in the brain that controls pleasure and motivation, similar to cocaine and heroin. That explains the pleasurable feelings experienced during smoking versus the craving, withdrawal, irritability, sleep disturbances, and cognitive problems during cessation. Approximately 72 million teens, ages twelve and older, use one or more tobacco products. The National Institute on Drug Abuse reported in 2006 that nicotine (in the form of cigarettes) has been the substance that the majority of high school students use daily.

Cocaine

Cocaine is the most addicting abused drug and transports the users to a stage of pleasure that is outside the realm of human experiences, but in the meantime, it may lead them into a world of *anguish* and even *death* due to *seizures, cardiac arrests,* and *internal bleeding*. Its psychological and emotional effects are perturbed and often paranoid. *Irritability, anxiety, depression, memory loss, mental confusion and violent behavior are among the many disturbances experienced by chronic cocaine users.* They betray their families and are a liability to society due to their delinquent behaviors and criminal violations. Unfortunately, there is research supporting that there are *eighth to twelfth graders that have tried cocaine at least once.* This is very alarming because many of our young people place themselves at high physical and emotional risks, without realizing the precarious outcomes. As we know, adolescence is a critical stage of personality development and the use of cocaine places the teens at high risk of maladaptive behavioral and psychological patterns in sociability and especially in interpersonal sensitivity, which appears to develop shortly after cocaine use.

Heroin

Heroin is similar to opium, codeine, and morphine. Our cell receptors in the nervous system, brain stem, and spinal cord recognize heroin and other opiates. These receptors trigger responses in the body and brain. Heroin changes the limbic system in the brain to produce increased feelings of pleasure and satisfaction. There are natural receptors in the brain, known as endogenous, that produce chemicals that act like opiates and control pain so the organism may survive under traumatic conditions. Brain cells are programmed to know how much to use of these natural chemicals. Individuals that use heroin recreationally often use much more than the brain would release even under the most intense circumstances. Therefore, this may cause increased pleasure and relaxation, and the user becomes dependent on it. Studies have found that heroin users and addicts suffer from *alienation, isolation, rebellion, depression, hysteria, schizophrenia and other psychopathic,* and *personality disorders.* Adolescents who are involved in the use of this powerful drug experience considerable disruption in their educational achievement and often develop a deviant identity.

Hallucinogens

Hallucinogens are psychoactive substances and are both naturally occurring and synthetically manufactured in the laboratory. Some of the illegal (recreational) hallucinogens that are used today are LSD (called Acid), MDMA (an amphetamine, called Ecstasy), GHB (Gamma Hydroxybutyrate), ketamine, mescaline, psilocybin or mushrooms, MDA (an amphetamine), and PCP (phycyclidine, also known as Angel Dust). The most popular hallucinogens among young adults and adolescents are LSD or Acid, psilocybin (mushrooms), DMT (dimethyltryptamine), mescaline (peyote cactus derivative), PCP or Angel Dust (phencyclidine), and MDMA or Ecstasy. The hallucinogens' effects are powerful and unpredictable on the brain. Some of the users may hallucinate and become aggressive and dangerous, while others may become drowsy and passive.

Hallucinogens are taken orally and their onset is relatively slow. In the inception of LSD, mescaline, and psilocybin, users experience nausea, dizziness, anxiety, and loss of coordination. Their vision is distorted and hallucinations follow. These delusions may be pleasurable and thought provoking for some, but for others disorienting or distressing, causing a negative emotional experience, known as a *bad trip*. As a result, the users may experience frightening thoughts and feelings of despair that often drive them to suicide. Long-term LSD users experience repetitious flashbacks for a long period of time after they quit the drug, as well as persistent violent behavior, anxiety, and distorted perception of time.

MDMA (Methylenedioxymethamphetamine)

MDMA or Ecstasy is widely used by college students; it is taken through the mouth and rarely is snorted. Ecstasy is produced in laboratories and is mixed with other recreational drugs, like PCP, heroin, crack, and even poison. Like other recreational drugs, Ecstasy detrimentally affects the users' physical, psycho-emotional, cognitive, and social functioning. Hyperthemia is considered the number one etiology of death among the Ecstasy users. It also causes liver, kidney, and vision damage. This psychotropic drug when entering the users' brain causes temporary euphoria (rush). However, the extremely fast deployment of serotonin depletes the normal serotonin (one of the natural mood enhancers) and produces dysphoria, anxiety, and insomnia. Ecstasy users continue to experience learning, retaining, and recalling difficulties long after they withdraw from the drug. According to the National Center on Addiction and Substance Abuse, by the time the adolescents reach age seventeen, approximately 47 percent will attend a party where alcohol/drugs, including Ecstasy, are used. Self-delusional teens are often lured to dangerous and raving parties, promiscuous and unsafe sex, and rape. They betray and abandon dignified friends for Ecstasy users. It is evident that Ecstasy as well as other recreational drugs continue to increase among adolescents and young adults. Only educational prevention will stop our youth from these threatening drugs, which are predators of our children's mind.

GHB (Gamma Hydroxybutyrate)

GHB, also known as the designer drug, is an odorless and colorless drug, which is ingested in liquid form but at times is available in tablets or capsules. Prior to becoming a recreational drug, it was used as an herbal supplement for insomnia, depression, and bodybuilding. GHB is a potent sedative drug, like ketamine and rohypnol, and even in a small dose can transfer the user into an unconscious stage. Professionals claim that it is harder to seize the addiction of this highly addictive drug than heroin or crack. Although researchers are not yet cognizant how this powerful drug affects the user, evidence proposes that GHB directly affects the brain's physiological mechanism that controls the release of chemicals and nutrients into the brain. Some of the users claim that they experience sexual and social enhancement and increased of energy. GHB is documented to cause hallucinations, confusion, memory loss, anxiety, and slow breathing. Many young users, being obsessed with the GHB habit, give up their educational pursuits, drop out of school, and become victims of drug dealers and other life misfits. It is time to reach out to save our youth by becoming anti-alcohol/drug activists in our neighborhoods, schools, communities, and cities or where the need is called for.

Ketamine

Ketamine is an anesthetic drug commonly used by veterinarians. Its recreational use started around 1980 and is sold as a dry white powder or clear liquid. It is one of the most powerful and psychedelic drugs, highly attractive to nightclub users and college students, is also identified as a high risk factor for *date rape*. Ketamine, like Ecstasy and GHB, has divergent effects, such as stimulant, anesthetic, and hallucinogenic possessions. Its users feel euphoric, insensitive to physical pain and distant from their surroundings. Violence, agitation, confusion, impairment in memory and learning are also associated with this widely used intoxicating drug. Ketamine is one of the faster growing drugs among our young people who prefer to use it over to Ecstasy.

The truth is that our youth are exposed daily and threatened by more and more recreational drugs as well other chemical agents. Our responsibility is to reach out and teach them how to keep drugs out of their lives.

Stimulants

Stimulants, known also as Speed or methamphetamine, are a powerful form of amphetamine. Methamphetamine is widely produced in illegal laboratories with highly toxic ingredients. In the 1960s methamphetamine was extremely popular but, due to its deadly effects, declined. Unfortunately, it reentered the alcohol and drug culture and increasingly became popular among adults and teens. Methamphetamine is a stimulant that acts upon the central nervous system. *Methamphetamine is highly addictive* because it enters directly into the brain's reward system whose neurotransmitters release excessive dopamine and work hard to absorb it. The build up of dopamine in the brain produces feelings of euphoria, which are registered in the reward system. Illegal methamphetamine users tend to use this drug frequently and heavily, which rapidly increases the production of dopamine. Methamphetamine damages the ability of the dopamine receptors to feel pleasure humanly, and as a result the users increase the dose to reach feelings of euphoria. Consequently, tolerance may develop rapidly and addiction occurs. Among the high risks that users face are: Cardiovascular complications, stroke, and damage of the brain vessels, high blood pressure, even death. Heavy users may experience paranoia, mood disturbances, hallucinations, hostility, anxiety, confusion, violence, and homicidal tendencies. The fact that stimulants are used as therapeutic and/or illicit drugs, we should be extra concerned about their intricacy and be well familiarized with these widely spread chemical agents before we consent for their therapeutic use.

Inhalants

Inhalants are chemical substances that fall into several categories, such as volatile solvents, gases, and volatile nitrites. Inhalants may be snorted, huffed, or gagged to produce intoxicating effects like alcohol. They are easily accessed and used by children between the ages ten and twelve years old. According to a Substance Abuse and Mental Health Administration's National Household Survey on Drug Abuse, approximately two million young people, ages twelve to seventeen, have used an inhalant in 2004. Inhalants harm the bodies and minds of users because they damage the fatty tissues that cover the nerves cells (neurotransmitters). Some of them depress the central nervous system and cause decreased respiration and blood pressure, while others increase the size of the blood vessels, allowing more blood to flow through. This causes damage in many body organs, including heart, liver, kidney, and adrenal gland. The inhalant users may experience headaches, nausea, and slurred speech, loss of coordination and consciousness, and even *sudden sniffing death syndrome.* Mental effects may include fear, anxiety, depression, or unpredictable behavior; memory impairment, attention deficits, and diminished non-verbal intelligence with chronic users. Heavy inhalant users tend to exhibit violence and delinquent behaviors and are ostracized socially. Lack of supervision, inconsistency in family life, peer pressure, easy availability, low cost of inhalants, and peer group pressure are some of the existing reasons that young people become involved with these perilous drugs. These highly intoxicating chemicals should be included in our educational agenda when we discuss alcohol and all other harmful drugs with our young children.

Anabolic Steroids

Anabolic steroids are hormonal substances that are chemically and pharmacoligically related to testosterone that promotes muscle growth. Anabolic steroid use has increased significantly among adolescents, who use them for building muscles and are purchased illegally in the black markets. The U.S. Congress has placed anabolic steroids as a class of drugs into Schedule III of the Controlled Substance Act. Steroids may be taken in the form of pills or injected directly into muscles. Abusers take doses 10 to 100 times more than what is medically allowed. Steroids cause cardiovascular and liver damage, elevated blood pressure, cholesterol, and premature hair loss in both boys and girls. Deaths have been reported from heart attack due to the arteriosclerosis, which causes fat deposits inside the arteries, among young athletes who abuse steroids. Studies also show that steroid users may have psychotic reactions, manic episodes, aggression, hostility, and violent behaviors. It is scientifically proven that steroids indeed present a high risk to our young people and especially to our athletes, who live in a highly competitive sports society that places great value on winning.

Indubitably the preceding information will serve as a reliable and valuable resource for your anti-alcohol/drug mission, but the knowledge of the etiologies, which drive our children to succumb to alcohol and drugs, will empower you to become more committed to anti-alcohol and drug advocacy. The causes of alcohol and drug use/abuse are multi-factorial and appear to influence each other in the manifestation and spread of this epidemic disease. In chapter 3, I identified these powerful factors under the categories of *esoteric, exoteric,* and *circumstantial.* Esoteric factors refer to genetic pre-disposition and psycho-synthesis (psychological make up) of the individual. Exoteric factors are related to the individual's environment—family, peers, school, and societal influences. Circumstantial factors are associates with individual's exposure to terrorism, wars, earth-quakes, and other natural disasters.

Researchers, through the study of pedigrees of large families with addiction, have identified genes and traits that predisposed offspring to alcoholism. Furthermore, there is reliable data that children born to alcoholic parents, even when raised by non-alcoholic adopted parents, have much higher rates of alcoholism than those with non-alcoholic origin. The latest research also indicated evidence of biological vulnerability to other drugs use/abuse, especially to opiates, halluci-nogens, and others. However, since drug addiction is influenced by multiple genetic factors, scientists today are focusing on biological and hormonal factors that make some people susceptible to addiction and not others. But there are still great individual differences in the neural structure of the brain and the production of hormones that make some individuals vulnerable to develop a chemical substance disorder and not others. Psychologists and biologists propose that individuals with *extraverted, neurotic,* and *psychotic* personalities are predisposed to alcohol dependency and other drug use and they tend to start at an adolescence age. Extraverts, being in constant arousal and boredom, need external stimulation in order to reach an optimal level of performance. Consequently they become highly impulsive and restless, which are empirically related to substance use. Children that are diagnosed at an early age with these traits exhibited alcohol dependency and other drug use in their adolescence years. Neurotic personalities experience highly internal distress and they often drink or use recreational drugs to medicate themselves. Psychotic personalities, characterized with traits of non-conformity, hostility, and impulsivity, tend to be at a high risk for substance use/abuse.

Treating young teens for a long period of time, I strongly concur that personality traits indeed have an alarming impact on the onset of alcohol and drugs, especially among adolescents, whether or not they are genetically predisposed to chemical substance. I also have confirmed that chemical substance use/abuse, for example, alcohol, cocaine, amphetamines, hallucinogens, opiates, cannabis, inhalants, and others, often triggers the onset of mental problems, diagnosed as

Psychiatric Substance-Induced Disorders. Examples of those conditions are mood and psychotic disorders, anxiety, sexual dysfunctions, and sleep disorders, all of which are of high concern to all professionals involved in treatment due to their comorbidity (co-occurring).

Among the leading and extensively researched exoteric factors are family, peer influence, school and societal influences. Researchers on alcoholism and other drug use support that parallel to genetic predisposition and personality traits, parental favorable attitudes toward drinking, smoking, or using other illegal drugs are associated with adolescent's initiating and continuing chemical substance use/abuse. Absenteeism of a parent, lack of family interaction and communications, inconsistency in parental direction or discipline, constant criticism, and the absence of parental recognition and praise all have been associated with high rates of alcohol and drug use among adolescents. Children of alcohol/drug environments tend to experience loneliness, isolation, poor-self-esteem, shame, and anxiety. In order to deal with these debilitating feelings, they seek relief through self-medication and consequently use alcohol and drugs. There is no doubt that family dynamics play a crucial role in the adolescent's direction in life, and it is a determinant to their participation in the alcohol and drug subculture.

Peer pressure has been recognized as an influential factor in adolescents' life decisions, especially in the use/abuse of alcohol and drugs. Adolescents that come from unsupportive family environments and experience feelings of alienations and despair are prone to succumb to their peers' perilous style, *use of alcohol/ drugs*. Peer conformity for social acceptance is another variable that lures adolescents to alcohol/drug use and abuse. Personally, I have treated many teens that have compromised their values and have become victims of drinking and recreational drug use in order to be accepted by their peers.

Adolescents that are not futuristically oriented and are not educationally motivated tend to enter the alcohol and drug world earlier than their successful counterparts. These aimless teens find more interest in alcohol and recreational drugs than in schoolwork and extra curricular creative activities that would deter them from alcohol and drug use and direct their pursuits in planning for a productive future.

Societal influences are not less responsible for adolescents' submission to alcohol and drugs, especially teens that are in conflict with the community where they live, and consequently they do not care for themselves or anyone else. Losing perspective of the future, they do not hesitate to seek gratification in the use of alcohol and drugs and other antisocial behaviors. The media, television, newspapers, radio, and movies often glamorize alcohol and drugs that influence the inquisitive minds of our children, who are not mature enough to recognize and differentiate harmful from nonharmful information. Undoubtedly, all this learned information would have a strong impact on their teen years toward alcohol and drug choices. Not to overlook the influence of the rap song lyrics, which contain lucid references to alcohol and other illicit drugs. The availability and easy accessibility to alcohol and drugs, especially with the manufacturing of a plethora of *designer drugs* (i.e., methamphetamine, Ecstasy, SLD, etc.) in the laboratories, allure teens to become early participants in the drug culture.

Poverty is another disturbing factor related to chemical substance abuse and use. Even low income Americans, who live below the federal poverty level, view drug *abuse* as a characteristic of poverty. That means that impoverished individuals are more likely to abuse chemical substances than their counterparts. There are numerous homeless adolescents that live on the streets of our metropolitan areas where survival sex and trading of sex for money or drugs is a daunting problem, especially among female runway adolescents. Indeed poverty plays an important role in the upsurge of teenage drug use.

Circumstantial factors include catastrophic events that associated with an individual or individuals' exposure to terrorism, wars, earthquakes and other natural disasters, altering human behavior and changing the course of life. Individuals that are directly or indirectly involved in some quivering situations experience a magnitude of stress reactions, known as post-traumatic stress disorders. Although stress is a common occurrence in the life of many people, it is also one of the most influential factors for chemical substance use/ abuse and addiction, following direct or indirect exposure to a traumatic event(s). Children exposed to severe stress, such as parental loss, child abuse, terrorist attacks, earthquakes, and hurricane experiences tend to demonstrate a strong relationship between psychosocial stress in their early life and substance abuse in their adulthood. Stress is also responsible for the release of the "corticotropin-release factor" (CRF). This is a hormone that initiates the responses to stress-stimuli. It is found throughout the brain and it appears to increase its levels in high-risk situations. It has also been found that alcohol and all abused drugs increase the levels of the CRF hormone. Thus, this suggests a neurobiological association with stress and chemical substance abuse. A national research followed after the September 11, 2001, terrorist attack in the United States revealed high prevalence of PTSD in individuals closer to the disaster and those actually in the building or injured. Although prevalence of PTSD decreased during the six months after the disaster, alcohol and substance use remained high. In addition, increased depression was related to alcohol, cigarette, and marijuana use. One year after the Oklahoma City bombing, there was reported an increase in alcohol use and marijuana. Stress and PTSD symptoms were also on the rise compared to citizens of other metropolitan areas.

Let us not forget that stress related to catastrophic experiences has an effect on people's entity, minds, and bodies. Furthermore, we should recognize that such disturbing experiences have a more harmful and damaging impact on our children and teens whose primitive defense mechanisms lack healthy strategies to cope with such stressful events. It is our responsibility to help our children and teens to acquire healthy defenses that will assist them to deal with the aftermath of painful memories of such devastating situations and events, which generate PTSD, a proven factor of chemical substance use and abuse.

Adolescents' early onset of alcohol and drug use often leads many defenseless teens to chronic or habitual chemical substance abuse and dependency. A 2005 survey revealed that half of the students in the United States tried an illegal drug before they graduated from high school. What is more alarming is that the teen's use of non-medical prescription medications, for example, Oxycontin, Vicodin, sedatives, and barbiturates rapidly increased. In addition, it is disturbing that adolescents involved in substance abuse are inclined to experience high incidents of psychopathology that will have a risky impact on successful developmental transitions. Among the many etiologies embedding the adolescents' alcohol and substance abuse are psychiatric disorders, childhood sexual abuse, and childhood behavioral problems. Alcohol abuse or dependence was found to be twice as high among adolescents who were diagnosed with anxiety, depression, and post-traumatic stress disorders (National Institute on Alcohol Abuse and Alcoholism, Youth Drinking: Risk Factor and Consequences). Childhood sexual abuse has been a predicator in the onset of early alcohol and drug use and initiation of injected drugs. It has been postulated from various studies that childhood sexual abuse leads to depression, substance abuse, re-victimization, and other internalizing/externalizing behaviors. It appears that the exposure to such paramount stressors in early life may be the mechanism through which early substance abuse and early-injected drug use occurs. Childhood behavioral problems, such as restlessness, impulsivity, aggression, and sleep issues in early childhood are also predictors of alcohol and other drug abuse in adolescents. Genetics, family dynamics, and peer influence, which are equally influential factors for alcohol/drug abuse, were already discussed in Chapter 3.

These findings are very alarming and when present require immediate professional help. Some noticeable warnings for immediate action may be: repeated health complaints and weight loss; inflamed and eroded nasal septum; lasting cough; low self-esteem; impulsivity; aggressiveness; threaten to hurt self; personality changes and defensive personality; selling personal or family possessions; running away from home and resenting authority; friends become top priority; problems with the law; changes to less conventional styles in dressing and music; decreased interest in school; drop in grades; and disciplinary problems.

Generally, young individuals do not identify themselves as problem drinkers or drug users. If you detect that your teens exhibit any of the above symptoms, it would be wise to have them screened and assessed by an alcohol and drug professional that specializes in adolescence. Among the various interventions implemented for adolescents' and young adults' alcohol/drug abuse is the *Motivational Enhancement Intervention* (MI), mainly used in the emergency rooms for drunk drivers, and the *Integrative Behavioral and Family Therapy* (IBFT). This model incorporates treatment for the substance abuse adolescents, therapy for their family, and behavioral and individual cognitive-behavioral therapy. Personally, I use the IBFT therapy with my teen patients, who find it motivational, entertaining, and didactic because through role-playing they learn to *cope with their cravings, solve conflicts and problems,* and a*cquire communications skills* to mange their anger, depression, and other negative moods. Do not regard alcohol and drug use and abuse as an adventure in your teen's life. Act upon it as soon as possible through early treatment services in order to stop the later pathological progression of alcohol and drug addiction, which frequently leads to the manifestation of substance induced psychiatric disorders.

As it has been discussed throughout this book, the stance that children normally take against alcohol and drug use is highly influenced by the role their parents, caregivers, teachers, and society play in their lives. I realize that there is not a hundred percent guarantee that children will or will not succumb to chemical substance agents, even considering traits, heredity, or societal influences. However, there are many preventive means and didactic ways that all those that are involved in the lives of children may use to empower the children's minds, bodies, and souls to make the right decisions and choose a healthy life, free from alcohol and drugs. *Good character*, the embedding of ethic values, the knowledge of goodness, value of goodness, and the inner drive to act upon it, has always been associated with alcohol/drug prevention and other negative and harmful behaviors. A person with good character possesses traits of high self-esteem, kindness, honesty, truthfulness, respect, responsibility, courage, leadership, citizenship, and other noble qualities. Children being in a constant learning mode have the ability to acquire all these desirable characteristics throughout their developmental years and use them later on for their life's decisions, including alcohol and drug use.

Some of the tools that may be used to cultivate and enhance good character in children are parent/caretaker and teacher modeling of high-self-esteem; responsibility and good communication skills; identifying and expressing emotions; preventing and controlling stressful events and situations that generate debilitating moods, which often lead to alcohol and drug use for escape and relief. Good nurturing and healthy emotions have been proven to facilitate and promote good decision-making in the prevention of alcohol/drugs.

There are other important variables that may rejuvenate children and adolescents' cognition, stabilize their emotions, and enlighten their minds in making the right decisions when they are exposed to alcohol and drugs. Researchers in the field of alcohol/drug prevention have found that good nutrition, sufficient sleep, exercise, relaxation techniques, meditation, and mindfulness work in synergy during the development and maintenance of a healthy body and mind, both armors against alcohol/drug use in adolescents' and young adults' lives. The *Journal of American Medical Association* reports that light to moderate exercise increases self-esteem, prevents anxiety and stress across all ages and especially in adolescents who are risk takers and often expose themselves to alcohol and drug experimentation. Mindfulness teaches self-awareness and can be a conscientious navigator in the adolescence life, which is often challenged by negative and harmful behaviors, for example, violence, crime, alcohol, and drugs. Mindfulness is a powerful tool of self-introspection that adolescents may use to discover their inner strengths and abilities and use them to make right decisions during the journey of their challenging lives, which are often enticed with the presence of alcohol and drugs and other destructive behaviors.

The school's role is equally important and crucial in the prevention of alcohol and drug use in our children's lives. It is recognized that the schools have always been strong advocates against alcohol and drug use through the development and implementation of educational programs, but it appears that there are a large number of students who are using chemical substance unthinkingly. As a former substance awareness coordinator in various high schools, I came to the realization that schools need more sophisticated and empowering programs, which predispose strong commitment to their delivery. That means, strong policies that reinforce a lifestyle free of alcohol and drugs for all students, regardless of their cognitive, psycho-emotional and social abilities, inspirations, and peer pressure. In addition, they need educators that are self-driven and are in control of their performance in order to inspire students to learn and recognize that alcohol and drugs are not an option of choice in their lives. It is an epidemic disease that is ready to take over their minds and bodies. Therefore, they must build anti-alcohol and drug resistance through good character, education, and personal commitment. School-based mental health and chemical substance prevention and intervention programs should be established where students may seek guidance and support for personal and academic problems that often generate stress and anxiety, both recognized triggers of chemical substance use for coping and relief. Peer-to-peer mandatory intervention programs should be available (starting in second grade) for high-risk students, who may draw strength from their sensible and caring peers, and thus escape succumbing to the internal and external temptations that may lead them to chemical substance use.

Our society needs to be accountable for our youth's alcohol/drug epidemic. Indisputably, our children's lives are in peril, not to mention the financial burden imposed on our society, which is associated with the astronomic expenses of alcohol/drug treatment, legal costs, educational prevention, and mental and physical illness as a result of substance abuse and dependency. Unfortunately, it is obvious that there is a denial as to the magnitude of the adolescence's chemical substance use/abuse problem. Consequently, our political leaders, judicial and human systems failed to take a drastic action to eradicate this paramount problem, which today has taken over the lives of our young people. Some of the reasons contributed to this frantic phenomenon are our laws pertaining to chemical substance traffic are not stringent and punitive enough; our judicial system does not harshly judge the chemical substance solicitors; the juvenile drug detention centers are not administered by competent individuals and they lack effective educational and therapeutic programs; the media's productions and presentations are not carefully censored by our government; and consequently there is a large number of hidden suggestive alcohol and smoking (cigarettes and marijuana) messages that encourage drug use. To make things worse, the FDA releases a substantial number of new drugs (potentially high for addiction) for marketing approval before are methodically tested.

Our government should take a fast stand and leading role in the prevention of alcohol and drug use by overcoming political rivalries and monitoring justifications. They must finance and encourage advocacy of anti-alcohol/drug groups to reach out to the high-risk young population and their families; finance schools to increase their alcohol/drug prevention programs; and develop free school-base intervention and treatment programs; demand the upper colleges and universities to incorporate into their educational curriculum alcohol and drug prevention programs for all potential educators and closely monitor and demand accountability from all state and federal funded youth detentions, alcohol/drug and mental treatment centers. Encourage and financially support all spiritual institutions to become advocates and educators of alcohol and drug prevention. Lastly, families, schools, and society in union should take part in this crucial and significant mission to create an environment free of alcohol and drugs, conducive to a healthy and productive life.

I conclude *How to Shield Children from Alcohol and*

Other Drugs in faith that you were enchanted by its noble purpose and that your minds and wills are empowered by its scientific and experiential information clearly and emphatically described in each chapter. Thus, you will be motivated and encouraged to pioneer against alcohol and drug use/abuse and inspire everyone else who is involved in our children's lives to join the crusade for an alcohol- and drug-free society.

References

Abadinsky, S. (2004). Drug Addiction and Drug Abuse. *The Columbia Encyclopedia*, sixth edition. New York: Colombia University Press.

American Academy of Child and Adolescent Psychiatry (2004, July). Teens: Alcohol and Other Drugs. Retrieved July 4, 2006. http://www.aacap.org/publications/factsfam/teendrug.htm

American Council for Drug Education's Web Site (2006, September). Signs and Symptoms of Youth Substance Use and Abuse. Retrieved at http://www.acde.org/health/signsymp.

Anglin, M.D., Almong, I.J., Fisher, D.G., and Peters, L.R. Alcohol Use by Heroin Addicts: Evidence for an Inverse Relationship. A study of methadone maintenance and drug-free treatment samples, Am. J. Drug Alcohol Abuse 15 (2):191–207 (1989).

Bailey, C.H., & Kandel, E.R. (1993). Structural changes accompanying memory storage. Annual Review of Psysiology, 55, 397–426.

Bandura, A. (1969, 1977). Mental Health: A Report of the Surgeon General www.surgongeneral.gov/library/mentalhealth/chapterr2/sec2

Bauer, J. (2006). Improve Your Mood With These Foods. Available at http://www.msnbc.msn.com/

Boucher, C. (2006, Sept.). Mental Illness and Substance Abuse. Retrieved at www.webmd.com

Branden, N. (2006). Health Self-Esteem. Available at http://www.nathanielbranden.com

Bremner, JD, Southwick, SM, Darnell, A., Charney, D. (1996). Chronic PTSD in Vietnam Combat Veterans: Course of Illness and Substance Abuse. *American Journal of Psychiatry* 1999; 153:369–375. Copyright 1996 by American Psychiatric Association.

Brown University Health Education (2004, May). Other Drugs: LSD. http://www.brown.edu/Student

CASA (2006) Teens Survey Reveals: Teens Parties Awash in Alcohol, Marijuana and Illegal Drugs—Even When Parents Are Present, August 17, 2006. http://www.casacolumbia.org

Cerebellum. Wikipedia. Retrieved August 4, 2006. http://en.wikipedia.org/wiki/Celebellum

Child Development Institute (2006, July). Television and Children: Guidelines for Parents. Retrieved at http://childdevelopmentinfo.com

Child Development Institute (2006). Raising Successful Teenagers. Retrieved July 6, 2006. Available at http://childdevelopmentinfo.com/parenting/teens

Child Health USA (2004): Population of Children. Department of Health and Human Services Health Resources and Services Administration, Maternal and Child Health Bureau. Rockville, Maryland: U.S. Department of Health and Human Services, 2004.

Cooper, M.L., Shaver, P.R., & Collins, N.L.

(1998). Attachment Styles, Emotion Regulation and Adjustment in Adolescence. *Journal of Personality and Social Psychology*, 74, 1380–1397.

Cornelius, M.D., Taylor, p.m., Geva, D., and Day, N.L. Prenatal tobacco and marijuana use among adolescents: effects on offspring gestational age, growth, and morphology. *Pediatrics*, 95: 738–743, 1995.

Flay B., and Sobel J. The Role of Mass Media in Prevention Adolescent Substance Abuse. National Institute on Drug Abuse Research Monograph 47, Superintendent of Documents, U.S. Government Office, Washington D.C.

Florida State University (2006). Sociologists Find Low Self-Esteem at 11 Predicts Drug Dependency at 20: Low Self-Esteem. *Journal of Child and Adolescent Substance Abuse*, April 5, 2006,11:58:36.

Focus Adolescent Services: Drugs and Teen Substance Abuse. Retrieved November 6, 2006 http://www.focusas.com/Substance Abuse.html

Green, S. (2006). Family Child Care Connections: Fostering Children's Self-Esteem. Volume 15, Issue. 2, 2006.

Guardian (September 6, 2005) Special K, the horse pill taking over from Ecstasy among clubbers. Retrieved August 31, 2006. http://www.ketamine.com

Harwood, H., Fountain, D., Livermore, G. (1998). The Economic Costs of Alcohol and Drug Abuse in the United States, 1992. Rockville, MD: National Institute of Drug Abuse.

Henquet, C., Krabbendam, L. Spauwen, J., Kaplan, C., Lieb, R., Wittchen, U-U., Van Os, J. (2005).

Prospective cohort study of cannabis use, predisposition for psychotic symptoms in young people. *British Medical Journal.* http://bmjournal.com/content/vo1330/issue7481.

Herd, D. (2005, Sept.). Changes in the Prevalence of Alcohol Use in Rap Song Lyrics, 1979–97. *Addiction*; Sept. 2005, Vol. 100 Issue 9, pp.1258–1269.

Holland, B. (1999, May). Government Reports On Drug Mentions In Music. *Billboard*; 05/08/99, Vol. 111 Issue 19, p73,2/5p.

Jason, L., Garber H. and Garber J. (2006). The Prevention of Depressive Symptoms in Children and Adolescents: A metal-Analytic Review. *Journal of Consultant and Clinical Psychology*, 2006, Vo1.74, No.3, 401–415.

Johnston, L.D., O'Malley, P. M., Bachman, J.G., & Schulenberg, J.E. (2005). Monitoring the Future national survey results on drug use, 1975–2004: Volume I, Secondary school students (NIH Publication No. 05–5727) Bethesda, MD: National Institute on Drug Abuse. August 2005. p. 397.

Katz, L.G. (1995). How Can We Strengthen Children's Self-Esteem. Available at http://www.kidsource.com

Kaufman, E. The Applications of Biological Vulnerability Research to Drug Abuse Prevention. In Biological Vulnerability to Drug Abuse, eds., Roy W., Pickens and Dace S., Svikis. Rockville, MD: NIDA, 1988, pp.174–180.

Khantzian, E.J. (1990). *Self-Regulation and Self-Medication Factors in Alcoholism and the Addictions.*

Similarities and Differences. Recent Development in Alcoholism, 8,255–271.

Kuhn, C., Sartzweider, S., Wilson, W. (2002). *Just Say Know*. New York: W.W. Norton & Company, 2002.

Kurtz, P.D., Kurtz, G.L., & Jarvis, S.V. (1991). Problems of Maltreated Runaway Youth. *Adolescence*, 26 (103), 543–555.

Loyola University (2005). Question Corner: Ask Anything You Want to Know About Drugs and Alcohol. Retrieved: August 16, 2006. hhtp://www.Loyola.edu/campuslife/healthservices/address/questions

Marlatt, G.A. & Gordon, J.R. (1985). *Relapse Prevention*: Maintenance strategies in the treatment of addictive behavior (lst ed.). New York, Guilford Press.

Maurizio F. (2006). Mind, Mood and Memory: 11 Vitamins for a Healthy Brain. Massachusetts General Hospital Letter, October 2006, Volume 2, No. 10.

McEwen B. & Lasley, E.N. (2002). The End of Stress As We Know It. (p.3). Washington, D.C.: Joseph Henry Press.

McGinnis, J.M., Foege, W. H. (1993). Actual Causes of Death in the United States. *Journal of the American Medical Association* 270 (18):2207–2212.

Measurement of Impulsivity in a Hierarchical Model of Personality Traits: Implication for Substance Use. Substance Use and Misuse (2006, Sept.), Acton, G.S., University of California, San Francisco, 2003, 38, 67–83 (PDF). Retrieved at www.personalityresearch.org

Messina N., Marinelli-Casey, P., & Rawson, R.

(Oct., 2006). Victims Without Voices; Children and Metamphetamine. *Counselor, The Magazine for the Addiction Counselors*, Vl. 16, 44–46.

Miller, p.m., Smith, G.T., & Goldman, M.S. (1990). Emergence of Alcohol Expectancies in Childhood: A Possible Critical Period. *Journal of Studies on Alcohol*, Vol. 51, 343–349.

Monti, P., Barnett, N., O'Leary, T., Colby, S. (2001) *Adolescents, Alcohol and Substance Abuse*: Motivational Enhancement for alcohol-Involved Adolescents, pp. 145–179, New York: Guilford Press.

Movaghar, A.R., Goodarzi, R.R., Izadian, E., Mohammadi, M.R., Hosseini, M. & Vazirian, M. The Impact of Bam Earthquake on Substance Users in First 2 weeks: Rapid Assessment. *Journal Urban Health* (Sep. 2005) 82 (3):370–7.

Muuss, R.E. (1996). *Theories of Adolescence* (6th ed.). New York: Random House.

National Conference of State Legislatures, Legislator's Guide to Comprehensive Juvenile Justice, Interventions for Youth at Risk (1996).

National Council on Alcoholism and Drug Department of the San Fernando Valley, Inc. (2006, July). Alcohol Awareness All Year Round. Retrieved July 4, 2006. http://www.ncadd-sfv.org/contact/newsletter.html

National Inhalant Prevention Coalition (2006, September). Inhalants: Social Consequences of Inhalant Abuse. Retrieved September 4, 2006. http://www.inhalants.org/guidelines

National Institute of Alcohol Abuse and Alcoholism,

Youth Drinking: Risk Factors and Consequences, Alcohol Alert No. 37, July 1997.

National Institute On Drug Abuse (NIDA)— Community Drug Alert Bulletin—Stress & Substance Abuse (February, 2002). Retrieved October 16, 2006. http://www.drugabuse.gov/StressAlert

National Institute on Drug Abuse, Mind Over Matter: Stimulants. Retrieved August 24, 2006. http://www.teens.drugabuse.gov/facts/fact

National Institute on Drug Abuse. (2006, July). Marijuana: Facts for Teens. Retrieved July 30, 2006. http://www.nida.nih.gov/MarijBroch/teenpg1–2.html

National Institute on Drug Abuse. (2006, June). The Science Behind Drug Abuse. Retrieved June 5, 2006. http://teens.drugabuse.gov/drnida

National Institute on Drug Abuse. (2006, September). Anabolic Steroids Retrieved September 7, 2006). http://www.teens.drugabuse.gov/facts/fact

National Institute on Drug Abuse. (1995, July). National Conference on Marijuana Use, Prevention, Treatment and Research. Arlington, Virginia. Retrieved July 30, 2006. http://www.drugabuse.gov/PDF/NJConf/MJTitlePage.html

National Institute on Drug Abuse. National Survey Results on Drug Use from The Monitoring The Future Study, 1975–1997, Volume I/Secondary School Students. NHI Publication No. 98–4345. Printed 1998.

National Institute on Drug Abuse. NIDA Research Report-Steroid Abuse and Addiction Retrieved September 7, 2006. http://www.teens.drugabuse.gov/facts/fact

Newhouse, E. (2006). Children Trapped in a Deteriorating Culture. Counselor: The Magazine of Addiction Professionals. Retrieved August 7, 2006. http://www.counselormagazine.com/display_article. asp

Nuttall, P. (1991). Self-Esteem and Children. Available at http://www.nncc.org/Guidance/self. esteem.html.

Ompad, D.C. et Al. (1997–1999). *American Journal of Public Health*, April 2005, Vol. 95, No.4.

Pilon, R., (2004). Peer Relationships: Who Are My Friends and How Do I get Kids to Like Me. Retrieved December 12, 2004. http://www.personal.psu.edu/users/j/g/jgp4/teach/497/peers.htm

Safety First. (2003). Facts about Drugs: Tobacco. 2003 Drug Policy Alliance. San Francisco, California.

Sapolsky, R.M. Stress, The Aging Brain, and The Mechanisms of Neuron Death. *The New England Journal of Medicine,* 1993, 329:1049.

Sharp, T.J. Relaxation Tips. Learn How To Feel Better: The Controlled Breathing Techniques. Retrieved December 4, 2006. http://depressionet.com. au/inspiration/relaxation

Smith, C. (2006). Focus Adolescent Services: How Can Parents Model Good Listening Skills. Retrieved November6, 2006. http://www.focusas.com/ListeningSkills

Smith, D., Christiansen, E., Vincent, R., & Hann, N. (1999). . Population Effects of the Bombing of Oklahoma City. *Journal of the Oklahoma State Medical Association,* 92, 193–198.

Spotts, J.V., and Shontz, F.C., Psychopathology and Chronic Drug Use: A Methodological Paradigm, Int. J. Addict. 18:633–680 (1983).

Substance Abuse and Mental Health Services Administration, 1999. The Relationship Between Mental Health and Substance Abuse Among Adolescents. Rockville, MD: Substance Abuse and Mental Health Services Administration.

Swan, G.E. (1999). Implications of genetic epidemiology for the prevention of tobacco use. Nicotine and Tobacco Research, 1 (Suppl. L.), S49–S56.

TelMedPak (2006). Alcohol. Retrieved July 4, 2006. <http://www.telmedpak.com/doctorss.asp?a=Poisons&b=alcohol

Tuprin, A., Tate, J. 1997 (1997). Mental Health and Homelessness. San Francisco Medicine (January).

U.S. Department of Health and Human Services. Healthy People 2010, conference edition, Vol. II, Washington, DC: USDHHS, 2000.

U.S. Drug Enforcement Administrations (2006). Drugs of Abuse Publication, Chapter 5 Stimulants. Retrieved August 24, 2006. http://www.dea.gov/pubs/abuse/5-stim.htm

Vlahov, D., Galea, S. Resnick, H. Ahern, J., Boscarino, J., Bucuvalas, M., Gold, J., & Kilpatrick, D. (2002) Increased Use of Cigarettes, Alcohol and Marihuana Among Manhattan, New York, Residents after the September 11th Terrorist Attacks. *American Journal of Epidemiology*, 155 (11), 988–996.

Waldron, H.B., Brody, J. & Stesnick N. (2001).

Adolescents Substance Abuse: Integrative Behavioral and Family Therapy, Chap. 7, pp. 216–240.

Waters, J., Roberts, A.R., & Morgen, K. (1997). High Risk Pregnancies: Teenagers, Poverty and Drug Abuse. *Journal of Drug Issues*, Vol. 27, no.3, pp. 541–562.

Whitebeck, L.B., & Hoyt, D.R. (2002). Midwest Longitudinal Study of Homeless Adolescents. Baseline Summary Report for All Participating Agencies. Department of Sociology, University of Nebraska-Lincoln, ND.